Endorseme

From Steven M.R. Covey

Art Barter is one of the truly great servant leaders in the world. As one who gets results in a way that inspires trust, Art genuinely models what he teaches. He's wonderfully captured his insightful approach to leadership in this fun and terrific book. A delightful read.

–Stephen M. R. Covey,
The New York Times and # 1 *Wall Street Journal*
bestselling author of *The Speed of Trust* and *Smart Trust*

From Cheryl Bachelder

A fresh, imaginative parable to challenge leaders to forget themselves and lead from their heart. When they do, the performance results will be stunning. And the pigs knew that all along!

–Cheryl Bachelder, CEO,
Popeye's Louisiana Kitchen, Inc. and author of
Dare to Serve—How to Drive Superior Results by Serving Others

From John C. Maxwell

Over the many years I've come to know Art, what I love most about him is that he not only teaches servant leadership, but he lives servant leadership. He has beautifully expressed his philosophy in *Farmer Able*, a story that takes the reader "down on the farm" to find the true satisfaction that comes from adding value to others as a leader. *Farmer Able* is an engaging story about a man who looked at his life and decided to lead in a different way. It is Art's heartfelt story, told with humor and wisdom. Read it . . . it will challenge your perspective.

–John C. Maxwell, NYT
Bestselling author and leadership expert

From Chris Stokes

The story is uplifting and inspirational and left me with joy and hope that we can change and make ourselves, our families, our businesses and all who we come into contact with better.

I had come to the end of the story before I realized that you had masterfully distilled an extensive body of academic literature on servant leadership, organizational development, motivation, and quality management to its essence and presented it in a way that may be used by followers, leaders, individuals, and families, from the smallest most remote undertaking to the largest global enterprises to improve their circumstances and outcomes.

–N. Christian Stokes, V.P. Business Development,
Victoria Mutual Building Society;
President, Jamaican Bobsled Federation;
four-time Olympic competitor;
author, *Cool Runnings and Beyond*

From Gary Ridge

Servant leadership is leading while serving others with the clear understanding that it's not about me. Art has shared how simple self awareness can unlock the passion of others.

–Garry Ridge, CEO,
WD-40 Company and coauthor of
Helping People Win at Work

From Bill Walton

My friend, Art Barter's first book, *Farmer Able* is really just the next step in his own remarkable and evolutionary journey of discovery, respect and empathy, that has delivered him, and eventually us, to the top of the mountain. Art has taken so many of the critically important lessons in life, transferred them into prose, and rolled it all into one, with this incredibly interesting, exciting, challenging and daring ride through the deepest depths of our souls.

The important principles of leadership that Art masterfully weaves through this dynamic story are the foundational pillars of the man who Art Barter has become, all the while leaving us to believe that we're just discovering all this ourselves.

Art Barter is a master teacher who is willing to do the hard things and make the tough choices that we either can't or won't do ourselves. *Farmer Able* is stocked full of the tools, the inspiration and motivation that will drive you to greater levels of performance, production and happiness.

This liberating and epic tale will change the way you think, dream and live. Do you care enough about yourself and the future to truly find out what is real, and what you can do about it???

Good luck. Hold on. Here we go!!!

And never forget that happiness begins when selfishness ends!!!

–Bill Walton

From Bill Driscoll

Great guidelines for living a kinder, more gentle life in today's 24-7, pressure-packed digital world. *Farmer Able* provides us with a fascinating series of easy-to-implement steps starting with an honest self-evaluation and ending with a can't miss formula for how to most effectively serve others.

–Bill Driscoll, Navy Ace and former TOPGUN instructor

From Olivia McIvor

Art Barter has crafted this entertaining parable that inspires us to seek the way of the servant; to find the courageous leader in all of us. This imaginative fable is stacked with humorous characters to engage us and to safely see ourselves while allowing fantasy to come to life with a profoundly powerful, yet simple message—*serve first*. Put all that together in this tale of life and work and you will find an inspirational read you can't put down!

–Olivia McIvor,
Bestselling author of *Turning Compassion into Action,*
The Business of Kindness and Four Generations—One Workplace
and an advocate for compassionate leadership globally

From Devin Vodicka

Art Barter is an inspiration to servant leaders and to those who have yet to discover the undeniable benefits of this powerful approach. His uncanny ability to crystallize important insights gained from years of experience and diligent study helps others to accelerate their own learning journey. Most importantly, Art models servant leadership through his actions. Through the combination of noble deeds and clarity of thought, he has earned a reputation as a champion for what is right and good in each of us, helping us to see within ourselves the amazing potential for collective transformation that is ever-present and often elusive in our lives.

–Devin Vodicka, Ed.D.
Superintendent of Schools,
Vista Unified School District

FARMER ABLE

by

Art Barter

Lead from
your hearts for
the sake of
others!

A
fable

about

servant leadership

transforming

organizations

and people

from the

inside out

Foreword by Ken Blanchard

Farmer Able: A fable about servant leadership transforming organizations and people from the inside out

Published by Wheatmark®
1760 East River Road, Suite 145
Tucson, Arizona 85718 USA
www.wheatmark.com

ISBN: 978-1-62787-235-5 (paperback)
ISBN: 978-1-62787-236-2 (hardcover)
ISNB: 978-162787-237-9 (ebook)
LCCN: 2014958689

Contents

Foreword...ix

Acknowledgements...xi

Introduction...xiii

Prologue... xv

1   Clarice the Cow...1

2   Harry the Horse 7

3   Juanita the Chicken...13

4   The Flummoxed Farmer 19

5   Foreman Ryder...25

6   Earnest Ernie...31

7   Patience 37

8   Sunny 43

9   A Little Secret..49

10 A Four-Stomacher...59

11 Sunny's Sore...67

12 A Whistle at the Knothole 75

13 Putrid Perfumery...83

14 The Mud Puddle...91

CONTENTS

15 Days of Straw and Sawdust...........................99

16 That Old Whip...105

17 Sparky..109

18 Growing Pains 117

19 Embraced by the Wind...............................123

20 Bubbles and Dishrags 129

21 A Sigh in the Henhouse 135

22 I Am Chicken..143

23 Listening to Be Heard 151

24 A Most Earnest Proposal...........................161

25 The Commitment of Pigs 169

Foreword

I've never owned a farm or even milked a cow, but this story spoke to me. Why? Because this little book shows why command-and-control leadership is a thing of the past. Like my good friend Art Barter, I believe that servant leadership is the only way to lead.

Our world is in desperate need of leaders who want to serve rather than be served. Organizations run by self-serving leaders are filled with demotivated people who spend their days protecting themselves and their jobs by bowing to the hierarchy.

Conversely, leaders who serve make it a point to catch their people doing things right and praise their progress. They join with their people to support not only the organization's goals but also each team member's individual needs. This creates an energized and motivating workplace where everyone works together for the greater good, achieving both great results and human satisfaction— a winning combination for success.

As a purveyor of simple truths, I can tell you one of my favorites: people who feel good about themselves produce great results, and people who produce great results feel good about themselves. Read this lovely parable and you'll see how servant leadership pays off for everyone—including the one doing the leading. When you make the conscious decision as a leader to serve rather than be served, you'll be amazed at what happens.

Thanks, Art. You're the best. Keep modeling servant leadership.

–Ken Blanchard,
Coauthor of *The One Minute Manager*® and
Leading at a Higher Level

Acknowledgements

This book has been made possible by the work of a great team of servant leaders. First and foremost is my family. My best friend and wife, Lori, has quietly influenced my own Farmer Able journey. My children, Jennifer and Chris, loved me at times when my behaviors didn't deserve it. Thank you for inspiring me to be a better husband and father. I love you.

The team at the Servant Leadership Institute (SLI) has been patient, supportive, and unwavering in its desire to get this project completed. Robin and Carol have been with me through the entire process. You continued to push me forward, ensuring *Farmer Able* reflects our hearts and desires to be better leaders in all aspects of our lives. Thank you for your servant hearts.

Matt and Jan Sommer took our experiences and stories and created *Farmer Able*. We could not have done it without your love for servant leadership and support for what we have been called to do. You have been patient, supportive, and creative, but above all your desire to serve us in ensuring our voice is heard has been a blessing we did not expect. Thank you for your servant hearts.

This fable would not have been possible without the help of my good friend, Ken Blanchard. When he spoke at my church, New Venture Christian Fellowship, in April 2003, he challenged me both in my faith and leadership behaviors. Thank you for helping me understand that servant leadership is not an option if I really believe what I believe.

I want to thank my close friend, Bishop Todd Hunter, for helping me get this book project started and introducing us to

ACKNOWLEDGEMENTS

Matt and Jan. Your love for God and desire to help others lead in a different way inspired me to keep moving forward.

My pastor, Shawn Mitchell, has shown me what servant leadership looks like in day-to-day behaviors. Thank you for your love for God and desire to be obedient.

To all those who have reviewed each draft of *Farmer Able* and took time to write such amazing endorsements, we are truly blessed to have such wonderful friends on this journey.

To the employees of Datron World Communications, thank you for joining me in the servant leadership journey, for embracing it and being willing to do the hard work of a servant leader. Together, you have and will continue to make a positive impact on lives throughout the world.

Thanks to all those who continue to inspire and equip servant leaders around the world. We are thankful to be on this journey with you.

Introduction

The following story is true. It's happening in businesses, families and throughout life around the world. I know because I experienced it firsthand in my company, family and circle of influence.

This journey began when I took a hard look at my own life. One of the most important things was to realize what I was doing wrong. Once I was willing to accept that, then the world of possibilities opened. Getting my team on board wasn't easy. But when they saw that I had given up my power agenda to better serve them, the floodgates of goodness, productivity and potential were released.

Yes, there are many challenges, but it is worth it. Inspiring and equipping others ultimately leads them to their own empowerment.

It also brings wildly unexpected treasures, filling both the heart and the pocketbook. Our company went from a bitter, backbiting $10 million pressure cooker to a self-giving, stress-reducing $200 million adventure. The bottom line: The way you get results is more important than the results themselves.

I trust you will find the truth in this story for your own situation—the wrongs that limit you and ultimately the rights that will multiply your efforts. I hope you and the people you influence each day will be set free to discover their own generosity of spirit and its many, unfathomable rewards.

I encourage you to lead with your heart . . . discover no limits. As leaders our role is to help others through the unfolding of life's events. Welcome to the farm!

–Art Barter
President & CEO, Datron Holdings, Inc.
CEO, Datron World Communications
CEO, Servant Leadership Institute

Prologue

I'm a witness. I've been there for it all. And now I've been asked to tell you about it: the many goings-on here at Farmer Able's farm. It's an old story that has been around since the hourglass of time turned over and it all began.

Some call me *The Land* or in a fruitful year *The Fields of Plenty* or just plain *Old Dirt*. I reckon that's what so many see me as. But what they don't see is what I've seen: not just the happenings, but also the manner of them. The hard rains of a spring, the dried out cracks during summer and the deep silences blanketed by the winter snow all conspire to give a certain perspective. Many a word, many a joy and even many a tear have passed above me and I've drunk them all in. I collect them like whisperings, precious and not to be forgotten.

Throughout, despite the muddying up or the drying out, I have a role to play. I give life—in the coming and the going of it, in the birthing, and even in the dying. So don't bemoan scrubbin' me out of your overalls after a workday or be embarrassed if I'm under your fingernails. I'm here for more than just to be worked. I'm here for the knowing and the seeing.

I'm a witness.

And what I've beheld on Farmer Able's farm has a certain wisdom to it—a truth as old as . . . well . . . as dirt.

It's all about me.

1

Clarice the Cow

"The pigs are running the farm!"

That's what Farmer Able grumbled to himself and even at times bellowed out loud.

This was the last thing any visitor might notice. After all, the pigs mostly laid in the shade doing nothing, so how could those lazy animals be running anything?

The only initiative they demonstrated was during feeding time. Then they sprang from their mud hole and oinked and squealed feverishly. Being fed by Farmer Able was all they were interested in. Just give them their slop and they were happy.

They were consumed by consuming.

But their piggish behavior didn't remain with just them. No, this attitude, Farmer Able believed, had begun to afflict all the animals on the farm.

"The pigs are running the farm," Farmer Able bawled as he went about his daily tasks. And everyone and everything on the farm began to believe it.

Clarice the cow saw how the pigs behaved. She thought, "Why those pigs do nothing and they still get fed. I have to go out into the pasture and work for my food. I have to eat grass and chew it over and over again. Then after all that cud chewing, I have to give over my milk freely. Of all the indignities!"

Every day Clarice grew ever more resentful, even jealous, that the pigs just lay there in their mud holes. As she chewed and chewed, each chew made her angrier. She thought, "I'm doing something." Chew, chew, chew. "They're doing nothing." Chew, chew, chew. "I'm doing something." Chew, chew, chew. "They're doing nothing." Chew, chew, chew.

And on and on her resentment grew.

Because of her great consternation over those pigs, she decided not to chew so much by eating less grass, which is a strange thing because she liked grass.

You could say she developed a cud-chewing disorder—a tick in her little cow mind. She thought smaller and smaller, and in her small thinking she produced less and less, which was really quite an "accomplishment" as far as she saw things.

She wanted to produce as little as those lazy pigs. Less was more to Clarice. She might have four stomachs, but darn if she was going to use them to their fullest.

Farmer Able had a little book he kept in the pocket of his bib overalls. He weighed each cow's milk every day and recorded it in that little book. He began to notice that Clarice was producing less. Clarice heard him muttering as he left the milk house. "Confounded cow. Her numbers are down. What is her problem?"

The accusation, "What is her problem?" made Clarice even madder. Even if it was her problem, she wasn't hearing any of that. She developed an "I'll-show-you" mentality. "I bring four stomachs to this enterprise and a lot of chewing to boot. Doesn't he know that? If he thinks I'm not producing enough, I'll produce even less and then let's see what he thinks."

Of course she didn't say this out loud. It was felt. And when an irritating thing like this is felt, it doesn't stay silent. The other cows picked it up. They experienced Clarice's irritation. They had to live and chew in the pasture with this very unhappy cow.

One young heifer named Bridgette tried to cheer her up. But even the cheering made Clarice angrier—because cheering up means you have a problem. And as noted, Clarice hadn't said anything, so she didn't like any fingers or hoofs for that matter pointed her way.

This, too, was a peculiar thing because Clarice had developed her own hoof-pointing. But she couldn't see it. It's the nature of hoof-pointing that the pointer is the last one to see it.

Having heard Farmer Able bellow about the pigs, she finally echoed this sentiment. "It's all on account of those pigs," is how she put it. "Those lazy pigs are getting away with doing nothing. Why, if I didn't have to walk by them every day, I wouldn't feel the way I do."

She also hoof-pointed at Farmer Able for his unkindly comments. He, too, was a major source of her rage. In fact, she came to think that her drop in milk production was entirely the pigs' and the farmer's fault. And now she could add Bridgette to that list as well. "I don't need any cow cheering me up because I'm not the one with the problem. She should look at herself. Her cheerfulness is because of her own set of problems that she's trying to overcome. And I'll have none of it."

So Clarice left the milk barn even more determined to eat and chew less. She missed the eating and chewing because that's what cows do best. Her four stomachs were definitely not full. Not only did this make her extremely hungry, but in addition, the whole thing gave her a sour stomach times four.

However, that didn't matter. She was willing to put up with these "sacrifices" because she felt Farmer Able was doing her a great disservice. He wasn't listening. His grumbling and complaining had made him deaf to her moos. In fact, she came to think he didn't care for her at all.

"It's all about me," was how she thought of his attitude. The poor cow didn't realize that same sour outlook had infected her.

Even the bell he'd hung around her neck came to irritate her. Before, she believed the bell and its sound were gleeful. It confirmed her place as part of the herd, as part of the farm. But it had become just a clanging in her ears. It reminded her of what an awful farm she lived and chewed on.

She imagined other farms and how wonderful they must be. But they were beyond the fence that held her in, so she didn't let her mind go there. She restricted herself. And she continued restricting her milk production.

Yes, the pigs were running the farm.

The whip makes
your team not pull
as a team.

2

Harry the Horse

"You think you've got it rough," Harry the horse said to Clarice, for he had heard and felt her complaining. "All you have to do is eat grass, chew and be milked. Farmer Able puts me in the harness and I have to pull the plow. Have you ever had to pull a plow? It isn't easy."

"That's what you're designed for," Clarice snapped back. "What do you care? That's your job."

So Harry, being angry at Clarice who was angry at the pigs, stopped working so hard. He fought Farmer Able when he tried to put on the harness. He fought him in another way once they got to the field: he moved real slow.

Farmer Able got mad at Harry and cracked him with his whip. And this wasn't just some little flick, either. He had never really had to use the whip before. But seeing this lazy, unproductive behavior, Farmer Able was obliged to make Harry work. In other words, he wanted the horse to feel it.

Like any horse, Harry certainly didn't like the sting of the whip. He'd respond at the initial crack, but then as he moved down the field pulling the plow, he would slowly ease up. He had to do this in such a way that Farmer Able didn't really notice. Yes, he was still in the harness. And yes, he was still putting one leg in front of the other. But was he pulling hard like his strong body was capable of? No. He didn't care to.

Little did Farmer Able know that the whip he cracked actually made Harry pull even less.

As he pulled less, the three horses in the harness next to him didn't know what to do. Even though Farmer Able might not have noticed Harry easing up, they certainly did.

This created a dilemma for them, because Harry was a very popular horse. Despite his lackluster performance in the harness, he really did "pull a lot of weight" with the other horses. Most of them loved saying they were his friend. You could even say Harry was the team's ringleader. The last thing they wanted was to be rejected by him.

Despite their frustration with Harry, they weren't about to whinny up and say anything. Such was the power he held over them. But they knew if they didn't keep things moving, they'd feel the lash, too.

A young, diligent—and you certainly could say naïve—horse named Jay cheered them on. "C'mon, we can do it," he said enthusiastically, feeling his oats. So they all hit the traces and took on Harry's extra load.

However, even if you're as strong as a horse, there's only so much you can pull. Their exhaustion and Harry's continued neigh-saying and plodding wore them down. Eventually, Jay tuckered out and started to reduce his effort. The others faltered as well. Gone was their giddyup.

Farmer Able was obliged not just to crack his whip on Harry's behind; he had to do it with the other horses on the team. Doggone it, if he wasn't going to whip all the horses into shape!

They certainly didn't like this. But did it even register that the sting was because of their lack of productivity? No, the culprit was Harry. He was the one who had brought out the whip.

"We're being punished because of Harry." Yet they had to keep this chorus of woe bottled up inside. They weren't about to speak out against the ringleader they thought of as a friend. So they just gnashed their teeth on their bits. A few thought they'd like to reach over and give Harry a swift kick. But they held back, and of course, Farmer Able's harness held them in check, too.

The result of all this holding back then whipping forward was a team out of sync. The horse cracked would lunge into the big collar around his neck and pull harder and faster for a moment— but the others would stay back at their slower, plodding pace. Then the crack would come to another to catch up to the horse who was pulling harder—but by the time the second whipped horse responded, the first was already beginning to slow.

The overall effect of this forward-backward, push-pull progression made the team … well, not a team at all. They weren't pulling the plow very well. Because they were harnessed together, they were pulling and heaving against each other. If you've ever had to drag a one-ton Belgian workhorse, it isn't easy.

They were lugging a double load. Needless to say, the field wasn't getting plowed efficiently.

"Confound it!" Farmer Able bellowed from behind the plow. "I paid good money for you horses. I calculated that you could plow two acres a day, but I'll be darned if we're even getting half an acre done a day." Again, Farmer Able was keen on numbers and productivity. "And yet, I still have to feed you the same amount."

Farmer Able regretted paying so much money for the horses. But what was he going to do? He needed the work done. To sell them now would get him further behind, and this was spring planting season.

Harry the horse was actually quite satisfied with Farmer Able's problem. He knew he had Farmer Able over the trough. "Yeah, he better feed me," Harry reasoned, "because without me, what does he have? He has a field unplowed and unplanted, which means no crops. And he has the audacity to whip me! If anything, he should be giving me a good rubdown every night for all I do for him."

Later that evening, as Harry chewed his oats he had a smug smile on his face. "That farmer thinks he doesn't have to listen and his whip can do all the talking. But we horses have the last word."

Yes, the pigs were running the farm.

When you coop up
a dream,
productivity
becomes a
nightmare.

3

Juanita the Chicken

Why even the chickens got into this conflagration. They, like the pigs, didn't have much to do all day. They didn't have to forage around out in the pasture for their grass. They'd just eat the grain Farmer Able threw at them every morning and evening in their chicken-wire pen just outside their coop.

No, what got them miffed was the day Farmer Able read an article in his *Advanced Farmer* magazine about how chickens could produce more eggs. The plan was simple. Don't let them run around in a pen. Put them in a cage. That way they could focus on one thing and one thing only: making eggs. All that energy running around outside wouldn't be lost. It would be concentrated.

So Farmer Able built out his coop with row after row of stacked cages. And he crammed the chickens into these little prisons. All the while he calculated the increased numbers of eggs he'd have, due to concentration, of course.

But one poor chicken named Juanita didn't like her new work space at all. She didn't concentrate on egg laying. A crack in the roof allowed the slightest ray of sunlight in. She couldn't see the source of the light; it was hidden by the roof on her cage. But its flicker illuminated, of all things, a dirt smudge on the wall before her.

Now you might not think something as cruddy as a grimy splotch would have any effect. But that small, shining spot—even as tiny and insignificant as it was—actually gave the beleaguered Juanita a ray of hope. She began to think that this flickering dirt smudge was really a portal to happiness. She could imagine a place on top of the barn where she'd be free like Ricardo the rooster to crow and crow and even command the morning. Or she would visualize a chicken paradise where she could fly like the robins and the barn swallows—effortlessly. Never mind that she had a big chicken body and little wings. No, that tiny crack of light, even if illuminating only a dirt smudge, allowed her to dream her chicken dreams.

She even fantasized about the pigs, who she knew were just sitting in the shade and slurping their slop. "Oh the life," she sighed. But that sigh turned to a chicken grimace. "Darn, if this doesn't grind my gizzard," she squawked. "Double gosh-darn those puffed-up pigs."

The other chickens didn't know what that comment even meant. They only knew the hatred they had for the cages and would simply squawk back at Juanita to pipe down. "It's hard enough being trapped in here," Peggy would say.

"Don't make it worse by your outbursts," Madge added with a certain pointed cluckiness.

So even Juanita's dreams turned to dark despair and depression. She squatted there in her cage as cooped up on the inside as her cage restricted her on the outside.

Her body didn't produce more eggs. Reality was an ever-tightening, ever-restricting existence that clamped off all those eggs.

Farmer Able kept track of his egg production in his little book. He was particularly interested now that he had invested so much time and material in his new cages. Expectations were high. But because all the chickens had adopted Juanita's mindset—and who could blame them—the egg production actually went down, not up.

"Confounded chickens," Farmer Able exclaimed. "Confounded *Advanced Farmer* magazine for telling me this new cage arrangement would make things better." Farmer Able was not happy. He cursed the day he got the cage idea in his head. But a farmer friend named Willis Achbaucher had an idea. He told him the chickens need darkness so they'll concentrate even more.

Farmer Able didn't think much of this drastic idea, but he had bragged a bit down at the grain elevator about his new chicken cage plan and how big his profits were going to be. He wasn't about to say the cage idea hadn't worked. So Farmer Able listened to his friend's advice and closed off the windows and doors. He let that little pot of chickens stew in the dark.

Yes, the good farmer had made productivity and profits his priority at the expense of the chickens' wellbeing. And everyone knows a consternated chicken doesn't produce.

The upshot of all this was that at night Farmer Able had dark dreams about eggs rolling out of the cages and smashing on the cement. Those profits he yearned for were turned to yolks and whites running down the henhouse floor.

So, while Juanita pursued vain comfort in a dirt smudge, Farmer Able was chased by nightmares about smashed eggs.

The pigs truly were running the farm.

A trust breakdown
causes
a rust buildup;
everything moves
slower and
costs more.

4

The Flummoxed Farmer

Farmer Able's poultry scheme had certainly laid an egg. And the horses continued to not work as hard, yet still eat as much. Given all this downturn, Farmer Able, being a practical man, got an idea. The cows always got a little feed when they came to be milked. The thrifty farmer calculated that he could make up the extra the horses were costing by reducing the grain he fed to the cows. After all, it was summer and they had plenty of green grass to eat in the pasture.

So he skimped on the cows' feed. But don't think the cows didn't notice. They have four stomachs to keep track of volume.

Clarice was the first to take note. Given her cud-chewing disorder and her self-imposed hunger campaign, she was really counting on that grain that was offered at her morning and evening milkings. The reduction released her full indignation.

She was so angry that she actually kicked Farmer Able when he tried to milk her. He wasn't about to put up with this. "Confounded cow!" he said, wincing. "What's got into you?!"

"What's got into me is less!" Clarice mooed in her cow voice that Farmer Able couldn't understand but all the other cows certainly could. "That's what's got into me. You think we don't see how you have us on rations. You tight-fisted skimper."

All Farmer Able could hear was a whole lot of mooing throughout this rant. Clarice was speaking, but Farmer Able wasn't hearing. Even if he could understand "cow language," the fact was it wasn't really a hearing issue. He wasn't listening.

Clarice's tirade got all the cows bellowing. Farmer Able could definitely hear their moans, but did he care? No, he walked, or rather strode back into the milk house and closed the door.

"Confounded cows. They can just keep all their bellowing to themselves," he griped. His snarls and surliness grew even more as he wrote down their milk production numbers in his little book. The numbers were dropping for all the cows.

But did Farmer Able equate this decline to his reducing their feed? No. After all, they were getting "plenty to eat" out in his pasture. This man—with the pencil he sharpened a couple times a day with his penknife—wasn't about to make that connection. No, he blamed it on things like, "Those darn cows!" and "The contemptible dry spring" (which wasn't that dry at all, but every year Farmer Able had to either declare a year more dry or more wet than any other year he had ever seen).

The one connection he certainly didn't make was the effect his grain rations had in quite another way. Clarice and the cows, who were smug about Harry and the horses anyway, now had even more reason to hate them. "You horses are the reason our grain is being restricted," Clarice said. This was true of course, because it was Farmer Able's prudent plan to borrow from one to feed the other.

Harry didn't care. He wasn't mad. He was glad to hear Clarice complaining. He had his feed and his loafing in the field and he was happy. Of course he hadn't stopped to consider that his malingering had made plowing twice as hard and half as fun because the other horses were pulling against each other. No, he took twisted satisfaction in just getting his due.

What he also didn't realize was that if this kept up, the fields wouldn't get plowed properly and on time. The crops wouldn't get planted correctly. The yields would suffer, and come next winter, there would be reduced grain for all the animals.

No, he chewed his oats contently for the time being. He couldn't perceive the gathering storm on the horizon. Even if he had thought of this, it would have been easy to quickly shift back to blaming Farmer Able.

Meanwhile, the chickens suffered as well. After all, the *Advanced Farmer* and Willis Achbaucher had said with the new cage arrangement, the chickens wouldn't need as much feed. They wouldn't be burning all those calories running around. What little they had would all go into egg production.

"Efficiency, that's what the modern farmer is all about," Willis had said. And Farmer Able, who certainly liked his sharp pencil, bowed at the altar of efficiency. The grand absurdity in all this was that the farm was anything but efficient. Farmer Able was so focused on the numbers that he had forgotten the true capital of the human . . . err . . . animal heart: trust. While the farmer was bent on the buildup of his enterprise, his uncaring ways were causing a trust breakdown. Without trust greasing the skids, it seemed that no matter how fast and hard he pushed, the slower and less productive everything became. Suspicion and downright ill will had worked its way in like so much rust.

The pigs heard all these goings on. Because they were pigs, it didn't bother them one way or the other.

When you think
you're the
big cheese,
all you do
is stir up
curdled milk.

5

Foreman Ryder

Farmer Able's troubles didn't end with all things fuzzy, furry and feathered. No, the chorus of complaint rose up from humans as well.

There was Foreman Ryder, who Farmer Able had brought in a while back to manage his affairs. The word "manage" was something Farmer Able liked to hear. It had a certain ring to it that gave this little country operation an air of importance. He could tell his fellow farmers who hung out at the grain elevator that he had "Ryder handling things." And this little fact, seeded into his conversations, placed him apart. At least that was the intent.

Foreman Ryder came with a resume forged in the school of hard knocks. He had worked his way up from a field hand. To hear him tell it, he'd spent many a year under the hot sun, in the sweltering haymow, in the freezing winters, in the cold spring planting and frigid fall harvesting. Ryder always thought of things in terms of hot or cold. And the more he told his stories about the arduous labors of his youth, the hotter or colder every rendition became.

Yes, he had pounded out a living busting dirt, and because of all his years paying his dues, he felt it was his right to bust heads.

The way he saw things, he had earned this privilege, and he made a point of making sure everyone under his charge knew it. Including the animals.

He slapped the cows to get them to hurry into the milk barn and whapped them to hurry out. With the horses, if they didn't behave, he'd get out the twitch. This draconian device had a small loop of rope secured to the end of a sawed-off shovel handle. He would twist it tightly around a horse's upper lip to get him "to behave." And the poor chickens . . . well, he could just pick them up and toss them where he wanted them to go. Yes sir, Foreman Ryder had not been spared from a hardscrabble life, and neither man nor beast should be spared either.

This caused even more obsessive cud chewing with Clarice, or rather cud-restricted chewing. Being a masticator, she couldn't stop her jaw from moving instinctively, even though her cow mind and downright bovine stubbornness had compelled her to eat less.

Out in the pasture she would moan, "The audacity of that man." Chew, chew, chew. "He thinks we're the beasts." Chew, chew, chew. "It's his behavior that's beastly." Chew, chew and double chew!

"Moo-wee!" Velma and the other cows responded. This sentiment always got a melody of moos from Clarice's fellow cloven hoofs. (With remarks like these, some even suggested making Clarice Committee Chairheifer of the herd.) Even Bob the bull, who always played the loner toughie, bellowed a stout affirmation, pawing and throwing some extra dirt up on his rump.

Harry the horse dreamed about giving Foreman Ryder a swift kick, but he knew this would bring out the dreaded twitch. So he came up with an ingenious plan. He acted the clumsy horse and simply stepped on Ryder with his giant hoof, pressing down as much of his bulk as he could muster. Ryder walloped him to get him to move, but Harry didn't mind the whack. He enjoyed seeing the foreman hop around smarting with pain.

Also, being the ringleader, he'd tell the other horses to slow down when they were called to come in from the pasture. Being late to the harness made him happy, if only to watch Ryder fume.

Juanita and her chicken friends became as clucky as possible, which means they set up an early warning system. The chicken nearest the door became the lookout. When she saw Ryder approaching the hen house, she relayed the message in her best bwacky code, "Cocka-doofus coming."

All Ryder's ears heard was the normal chicken cackle, to which he responded, "Pipe down you bunch of bird brains."

But this only made the chickens on down the line cluck more, "Cocka-doofus . . . Cocka-doofus!" This little amusement lifted the beleaguered Juanita's spirits. Everyone knows that for a chicken, intermingling clucking with chuckling is quite the poultry pastime. Mocking Foreman Ryder was all fine, feathered fun!

Farmer Able was largely oblivious to this ill-tempered woe. He welcomed Ryder's "git-er-done" attitude—at least at first. But as anyone knows, hiring power inevitably creates a power struggle. Though Foreman Ryder knew the hierarchy of things, in the grimier recesses of his mind, he certainly didn't embrace it. A man who feels a need to lord over another inevitably smarts under the one who is over him.

Ryder's paycheck, of course, kept his rebellion in check for the most part. But that didn't keep him from an attitude of superiority. He actually felt Farmer Able should be working for him. He came to believe that without him, Farmer Able's entire operation would be in shambles.

Yes, Foreman Ryder's sniveling self-importance gave him a sense of great power. He never stopped to consider that he hadn't put together his own operation and taken any risk to be his own boss. No, he was content to cop the attitude that he *should* be running things, even though to own and run something he would never do. No, to hear him tell it, he was the victim of unlucky breaks: of those tight-fisted bankers who wouldn't give him a loan . . . of those conniving schemers who had blown into his life and drained his resources . . . of life itself, that always seemed to deal him a raw hand. All those forces had conspired to keep him from being the captain of his fate.

Yes indeedy, fortune never smiled on poor Ryder. And he was going to make sure it didn't fall on any under his charge, either. His outlook had become just like the pigs, who were content to plop down, mired in their mud holes.

Caring for others:

weakness

or

strength?

6

Earnest Ernie

Regrettably, much of Foreman Ryder's fury was visited on Ernie, the hired hand. Ernie was a good-natured fellow who had an easy-going, humble way with people and with the animals. Most people liked Ernie. However, it was this very meekness that was despised by Foreman Ryder, and even Farmer Able. They saw kindness as weakness.

"'Ah shucks is okay for some hick in the funny papers," Ryder would grouse, "but I don't want to hear it or even sense it at this here operation." Ryder liked to refer to his job as the "operation" because it added extra importance to his position. Ernie wanted to point out that saying "this here operation" had a certain hickish ring to it, but it wasn't Ernie's way.

Actually, Ernie wasn't quite sure why the "ah shucks" bothered Ryder. Ernie was just being himself, which meant he was being responsible to kindness and other good things like looking out for the wellbeing of the animals, working hard, and even letting other people pump a drink of water before he did.

As for their work, Ernie and Ryder saw things quite differently. Ernie considered a big part of his job being what he called "fussing over things." After a long day's work in the field, he'd give the horses a little extra rubdown with the curry brush, or he'd stroke the udders on a cow and pat her soft brown hide. He thought this coaxed out the milk better. Even with the chickens, he'd try speaking in "chickenese," letting out his own version of "Coo-karoo, coo-karoo."

The lookout chicken, when she saw Ernie coming, would give a cluck report. It went something like "Bwahk-bwahk . . . bwahk away . . . Cock-a-doodle coming."

Yes, the chickens referred to Ernie as "Cock-a-doodle" because he seemed to them to be a bit peculiar. They had been so beaten up by most of their human interactions, that they had trouble understanding him. His kindheartedness was suspect. After all, isn't caring in a person just a little questionable? "Why he's just appeasing us," Peggy squawked. "You just wait. He'll be the first to ring our necks."

Being caged and abused created all manner of brain fatigue in their little hen heads. They weren't seeing things clearly. Even when Ernie would reach out simply to pet, or heaven forbid, hold a chicken, they became—like their distant cousins—a bit goosey. They'd retreat to the very back of their cage and even peck at Ernie's outstretched hand.

They, too, had come to view his kindness as weakness. In fact, they saw him a bit like themselves: a chicken. To anyone schooled in chicken psychology, this was projection plain and simple: I'm a chicken; you're a chicken.

Ernie was at a loss to understand this behavior. He kept figuring that if you're just kind to everyone—including the feathered and certainly the featherless—they'll be kind back. He didn't realize he was fighting a losing battle.

The situation Farmer Able had created, cooping up the chickens in the cages, was working against all of Ernie's noble intentions. He couldn't override it. And Foreman Ryder's harshness when he came storming into the henhouse further branded the chickens' psyches with great consternation and repulsion to all things human.

Ryder, in yet another twisted demonstration of power, liked to wave his hand fiercely toward the chickens just to watch them jump. "You bunch of chickens," he would say, thinking his play on words was funny. The irony was that in Ryder's warped mind, what he stereotyped as a chicken was completely confirmed. Chickens really are chickens, he deduced.

Ernie would never believe this. Even though he saw them scurry to the corner of the cages, Ernie had an understanding—a chicken relatability. He knew somewhere deep in his own heart that despite Ryder calling him names like "chicken"... he wasn't. And he naturally thought the actual chickens weren't, either.

Yes, the pigs were running the farm and the selfish behavior that ensued couldn't even be pierced by caring for others.

When priorities
aren't right,
those most
important
to us suffer.

7

Patience

These were the goings-on out in the barn lot. But the mess out there spilled over into that would-be sanctuary: the home.

Farmer Able's beautiful bride, Patience, had gleefully embraced the role of farmer's wife. She not only made the house a welcoming abode, she also put many an hour in the milk barn, the fields, the calf pens and even at the working end of a manure fork. She had welcomed newborn things of every hoof and horn into the world, even feeding from a bottle if necessary.

All the while, she still managed to add a little splash of fresh-cut flowers or crisp gingham drapes to bring color and warmth to the farm. This able-bodied woman also didn't shy from rolling up her sleeves and offering a hand to neighbors who were suffering hard times. Yes, Patience was an integral part of the grand scheme of things on the Able farm. This prudent pioneer was mother, wife, high counsel and frontier warrior.

She certainly knew Farmer Able long before the years of worry had piled up on him. He had vibrancy, a skip in his step, like the colts in spring. Yet, as the cares came, it was as if he took up a great sack and filled it one-by-one with rocks. He dragged this burden around unseen but never unfelt. Patience believed that somewhere under that load, a certain abandon was still there. If only she could help him unburden himself.

Somewhere along this arduous journey, Patience had stopped being the main priority. Oh, Farmer Able would say she was tops on his list. But that old squirrely friend, "rationalization," would work his dark magic, and Patience was simply put on the back burner.

Even though her name was Patience, Farmer Able's volatility had worn the stalwart intent of that name quite thin. After months and even years of Farmer Able's outbursts and depressions, her own flame of enthusiasm fought to flicker. In a sense, she was like a barometer. She could feel the ill winds in the emotional weather. However, being an honest person, she wasn't about to withdraw from these climate fluctuations. To Patience, sweeping a matter under the rug, even if stormy or a little messy, was only creating a bigger problem later.

She addressed Farmer Able's tantrums in accordance with her name. Yes, she would tolerantly endure his grousing. But patience doesn't mean being a doormat. Actually, her plan, though not always conscious, was to speak the truth, then "patiently" wait for her sour-minded husband to see if he could grasp it.

Many a sentence would begin with, "Have you considered …" But Farmer Able's head had become as hard as the old oak beams in the barn. Stubbornness wears a lot of armor. The man simply couldn't see a way other than the "way we've always done it," … or … "the way things ought to be," which is to say he couldn't see a way other than his own.

"Confound my name," Patience cried out once when she was alone after yet another surly flare-up from her husband. Patience's outpouring was directed at no one in particular, save the great silence around her. It came with tears. People who are pressed between what can be and the harsh realities of what is have little choice but to have tears squeezed out of them.

Farmer Able's outbursts put a strain on their relationship. Oh, how Patience could be a comfort, yet Farmer Able was inconsolable. Oh, how Patience could offer expansive wisdom, yet the farmer had restricted his brain to think small. Oh, how this wife of his youth could be a spring of youth-restoring vigor and life, yet the man was hell-bent on picking through the same-old-same-old.

She believed in a greater goodness, even though the farmer with his sharp pencil, calloused hands and sweat on his leathery neck often seemed only to believe in his worries. Behind his hard-headed eruptions and behavior she knew there was a man with a soft heart.

So Patience endured, waiting for a spark of hope.

Yes, Farmer Able had allowed those pigs to sit themselves down squarely in the middle of their relationship.

Are you listening

to what you hear?

8

Sunny

Farmer Able's daughter, Sunny, certainly had a natural cheery disposition, brimming with enthusiasm. Yet when it came to her father, she wasn't as tolerant as her mother, Patience.

Generally speaking, Sunny was like a summer sky: sunshine most days, with the occasional storm. She was a teenager and spoke all things as they came to her mind. And sometimes these were quite emotional.

Farmer Able didn't understand these outbursts. He remembered Sunny as the little girl who loved to ride with him behind the horses in the field. He bought her ponies and helped her raise lambs for the county fair. Where did those drops of sunshine go?

Sunny had a constellation of friends and loved to hang out with them down at the local root beer drive-in. At school, she was quite involved. She got good grades but was also engaged with many extracurricular activities. Her favorite was theater, even if she only got small parts.

Yes, the sweet life outside the confines of the farm couldn't have been sunnier for Sunny. However, her dad's behavior ensured a certain overcast reality back at the Able homestead. His bitter disposition had all the rancid taste of leftover milk left to sour in the sun. They fed this curdled concoction to the pigs, who slurped it gleefully.

She heard her dad hollering at the cows. She watched him flicking the horses to get them to mind. When she gathered eggs each morning (one of her daily chores), her dander would get on up when she saw the dark coop in which her father had imprisoned her feathered friends.

On more than one occasion, she would take a hen out into the sunlight. One time she managed to grab Juanita. The frightened feathers quivered in her hand, but Sunny would coo, "See the sun. I'm named after it. Don't be afraid. The warmth and vitamin D content will do you good."

Juanita in her caged-up state only understood the terror of what a human hand could do. In the grip of a human, she didn't grasp Sunny's goodwill—let alone the vitamin D comment. In a sad, strange twist, Juanita actually welcomed getting put back into her dark little prison. If kept in darkness and smallness long enough, a chicken—and certainly the chicken-minded—will embrace even a horrible thing. They'll welcome the confinement simply because it's what they know and what they think knows them. It can quickly turn a free-enterprise mentality into an institutionalized mindset.

These mistreatments coming from her father built up in Sunny's soul, like a dam holding back water. Oftentimes, Sunny felt like her father served up the same rottenness to her. This mounting energy was such that when her father came in and berated her, saying "You need to sweep out the cow barn better (another one of Sunny's chores)," or even "I want you home by 11," the dam would break.

Her reaction brought out an even greater overreaction from Farmer Able. And the floodgates of temper were unleashed on both sides.

Patience tried to intervene, but anger breeds rage and rage

looks for victims. Her appeal to "seeing the other side" was met with wrath heaped on her head. Both husband and daughter took liberty to give Patience what for. Fury can be a club, and once people take it up, they'll use it on anyone whose lips happen to be moving.

The blowups between headstrong father and strong-willed daughter always seemed to end with the two boxers retreating to their respective corners. Sunny would storm up to her room and revisit the outrage over and over again.

As far as she was concerned, her father had two ears but only one stubborn way of thinking. He simply wasn't listening. When people are fixed on what they'll say next, they certainly aren't hearing what someone is truly saying now. Their need to open their mouth actually closes their ears.

Yes, the pigs running the farm could just as well have made the farmer's home their personal sty. After all, their all-about-me attitudes had come to permeate this sorrow-filled refuge.

It's not about me.

9

A Little Secret

Most evenings, given all this turmoil, Farmer Able would withdraw to his office and sulk. This hovel was really nothing more than a ramshackle little space just off the old granary. It had been used as a tack room. The smell of oiled leather still permeated the walls and conspired with the musty whiff of grain dust. The farmer had cleared out all the harnesses and moved in an old oak desk. He had added an ancient upholstered chair for a bit of comfort, though the stuffing was starting to come out in places.

In this oily, oaty shack, the farmer would lay out his bulky ledgers. He meticulously transferred numbers from the little book in his bib overalls' pocket to the hefty registers. The farmer found strange comfort in the ruled pages as he ground his pencil ever sharper and wrote out the pluses and mostly minuses of his accounts. He stored the ledgers, marked year-by-year, in file cabinets that stood like metal testaments to his many failures. His less-thans and could-have-beens were committed to ink and paper and encased in steel.

This simple little exercise of keeping his accounts was exhausting. Every entry took a heavy toll. The good farmer spent so much time worrying over the numbers that the only thing that was adding up was his anxiety. His overworked mind—not to mention the day-to-day grind to get all his jobs done—would regularly cause an overstressed stomach. Farmer Able had developed a persistent bellyache.

While Patience always made a nice meal, her husband rarely sat down with the family. He would take his plate of food to his office and eat even as his worry ate at him. On more than one occasion, his gurgling gut wouldn't even allow him to finish his dinner. This evening was no different, and he had pushed back his plate half-eaten.

Now you might not think that Clarice's pooh-mooing and Harry's neigh-saying and even Juanita's consternated clucking made a bit of difference. However, those pleadings didn't fall on deaf ears—leastways not on a farm, for a farm has a certain bonding. These bemoanings had a way of shaking the very foundations of a place.

Whether it was due to those plaintive moans of hoof and horn, or simply the grander designs of the universe, a most peculiar thing happened one particular evening.

As Farmer Able stared at the penciled numbers, trying to avoid the acid in his stomach, he noticed something quite strange. The old barn siding, which had become weathered over the years, always had a creaky sound to it. However on this night, the spring wind that blew outside conspired to create an odd whine and wail as it forced itself up against the old boards.

Moan went the wind, then *groan* went the boards at an even higher pitch as the gusts accelerated. The effect was like breath across the reeds of a harmonica. Adding to the sound was a sing-songy whistle.

The farmer put down his pencil. He just had to fix that irritating sound, so he went outside and stumbled along the shed trying to locate the shaky boards. However, he could find nothing that fixed the spot of the strange reverberation.

With one particularly strong gust of southern wind, his attention was turned to an even more unusual creak. It came from the old walnut tree standing as it had for some 80 years in the lot just outside the granary. The *moan* and *groan* were even more pronounced in the tree as the branches moved in the wind. It had a distinctive tone to it that the farmer hadn't heard before. The sound went beyond a *rustle* or even a *swoosh*.

Adding to this display was a light dance on the tree itself. The full moon that shone down that night lit up the old walnut with a curious luminescence. The branches were silvery and appeared to glow.

Farmer Able thought "what the dickens?" as old leaves left over from autumn swirled at his feet. There appeared to be something stirring, a conspiring of sorts between wind and light and tree. As he stared dumbfounded, the sounds took on even more definition. From *creak* and *moan* . . . to *oooh-weee-oooh* to *aaaa-ble*.

Did the wind just say his name?

And then—*sweet molly moonlight!*—Farmer Able heard a most distinct English word: *It's*.

The word faded with the wind. The farmer wiggled a finger in his ear. Surely he wasn't hearing what he was hearing. He was about to leave, when suddenly the wind gathered itself again, and through the branches came words with even more particularity: *It's . . . not . . .*

Accompanying the words was that unmistakable twinkling from moon to branches. The sounds of the words were in rhythm with the pulse of that light. The articulation came from the wind, across the tree, and then it resonated on the creaky boards of the granary. He was hearing it coming and going, inside and out.

It's . . . not . . . about . . .

The wind sound trailed off like it was taking a breath. Then summoning itself again, a gust built up.

It's . . . not . . . about . . . me.

The reverb echoed off the granary: . . . *about* . . . me . . . me . . . *me*. The wispy resonance faded into the night.

Suddenly the wind stopped dead. All was still. Farmer Able just stood there in the silence. Mysteriously, he could still hear the words inside. However, he shook his head and let out a deep breath. The forceful exhale caused his cheeks to sound like Harry when he snorted.

"Bah!" he said out loud, as if talking to a fool. He let out a belch, which reminded him yet again of that sour stomach and his even sourer mood.

He strode back into the grimy confines of his office and sat down. The ledger pages of neatly displayed numbers stared up at him. He gathered himself. These concrete figures would bring him out of his stupor . . . or so he thought. The farmer grabbed up his pencil, ran it through the sharpener just to put a fine point on *reality* and started in again with recording his figures.

As he sat there, the wind began to pick up fiercely. This time the gale did not stop at the walls. It found one particular knothole and pushed at its rotten center until the knot actually popped out. The farmer could now hear the wind whistling inside his office.

After a moment, an endless stream of ants came through the knothole. They made their way down the wall, across the floor, and up and across Farmer Able's desk. Like all ants, they formed a magical line, marching to a decidedly determined purpose. They paraded right over his ledger book.

As the farmer watched them, two lines formed: one coming

and one going. The coming ants would pause ever so briefly to touch antennae with the going ants to download some ant whisper that steered them on an exact course.

Farmer Able's glossed-over eyes swam trying to fix on this resolute line of energy, entering desk left and exiting desk right. Like a subject watching a hypnotist's swinging watch on a chain, Farmer Able became spellbound.

At first he didn't mind that they were swarming over his neat lines of debits and credits. They scurried quickly and left no mark. For a moment he rather enjoyed their industry. After all, Farmer Able was a man who prided himself in his own hard work.

But then the farmer came to his senses.

He brushed the ants off his ledger and desk. After this flurry, he slumped back in his chair and momentarily closed his eyes. Yet when he opened one eye, and then the other, he saw the ants were back. He may have disrupted the middle of the chain, but there were many comers and goers who had immediately filled in the two lines.

A determined thought entered his mind: *They're after something or they wouldn't be here.* So he followed the marching ant line. To his horror, they had found his half-eaten plate of food. They were determined to finish off what Farmer Able couldn't.

Farmer Able wasn't about to let them make a meal out of his dinner. He moved the plate and began an even more furious sweeping and flicking and wiping and clearing. Yet as anyone who has tried to get rid of ants knows, where there's one, there are a thousand. The more he cleaned, the more they charged—wave after endless wave.

Farmer Able was fighting a losing battle. He finally succumbed, falling back into his desk chair. This time he didn't shut his eyes and pretend they weren't there. No, he sat there with his bleary eyes opened and transfixed, watching the foes that had vanquished him resume their determined march. They were after every little crumb.

The depleted man scoffed at himself pathetically, "You beat me. Why, I can't even win over you measly ants." At that moment the proud farmer felt even littler than the ants. As he sat steeped in this misery, another thought percolated up from his soul. It came from the very darkest place. He murmured out loud: *Somebody help me.*

It was at this point—lower than a deep well drilled that produced no water; lower than a sow's belly dragging through the pigsty muck—that the wind kicked up again. It whistled through the knothole, expressing that mysterious phrase: *It's not about me.*

As the farmer focused on those ants, the words took on new import. The ants were the living embodiment of that thought. Their lack of complaint and their unflinching resolve were certainly not about them at all.

The farmer took his pencil and jotted down the phrase in his ledger book: *It's not about me.* The busy ant lines streamed right by it, their wiggly march seeming to animate the words.

But then a potent emotion welled up within the farmer. He wasn't sure why, but the ant trek began to anger him. Maybe it was because they were crawling across the entries in his ledger. Even though they carried on, oblivious to the farmer, he took it as if they were mocking his dismal finances. He couldn't figure it out. All he knew was that the cryptic sentence, that vexatious wind and those pesky ants were anathema to him.

His fury erupted. In one heated swoop, he flung the ledger off his desk. He got up abruptly to leave. But in his haste, his foot caught on a toolbox he had left open on the floor. He stumbled and fell, hitting his head on the metal filing cabinet on the way down, knocking him out cold.

As the farmer lay there, the ants simply reestablished their lines and resumed their vigilant parade.

My anxiety gives

everyone else

a stomachache.

10

A Four-Stomacher

The next morning, the sun came up brightly, but the fog in Farmer Able's brain didn't lift. He not only had to deal with his queasy stomach, but he now had a throbbing goose egg on his forehead from the fall.

"What happened to you?" Patience asked as she served him his black coffee and fried eggs.

"I tripped," was all he said.

Patience drew out an "Ohhh-kay ..." not content with this obvious answer. Then as she stirred her coffee, allowing the silence of a country kitchen moment, she followed with, "How come you tripped?" She took a sip looking into her cup as she said it.

Farmer Able knew what she was after: a full confession. But he wasn't about to offer this up. So he grumbled a half-truth: "Confounded toolbox. Didn't see it." The toolbox, of course, was the "truth" in the equation, while not divulging his anger was the "half."

"Uh huh," Patience responded, knowing that the unspoken thing was the real answer. "You'll have to be of a mind to pay more attention. You know you might just consider you're a little over-worked and overstressed." And she got up from the table to do the dishes.

Farmer Able knew what her "be of a mind" comment meant. He also knew deep down that he was overtaxing himself. But he wasn't in any state to embrace any of this. That would mean his mind would have to be an open one, and the good farmer's was hammered shut. He left his coffee and most of the eggs, his gurgling gut issuing a resounding reproof.

The blaze of the dawning sun hit him as he strode out into the barn lot to start his chores. This only increased the throb in his head. With that pounding and the lingering nausea, even the slightest provocation would set him off.

The first incitement was Ernie. "Mornin' Able," the gleeful hand said as the farmer stepped into the milk house. Ernie had already been busy putting the milkers together. The singsong in Ernie's voice was particularly irksome. "Cows are in their stanchions, ready to get the moo juice flowin'." Farmer Able only grunted. Sensing the farmer's surliness, Ernie attempted to brighten the mood. Addressing the cats, he said playfully, "I bet you all can't wait for some warm milk."

"No they can't," Farmer Able groused. "So let's get to it. Quit jawin'."

Ernie felt the rebuke. He started to grab a milker and head into the milk barn. But Farmer Able took the milker from him. "I'll do that!" the farmer said. Ernie wanted to point out the inconsistency in these two requests, but seeing the goose egg on the farmer's head, he thought it best to let the incongruity slide.

"I'll do the milking this morning. You tend to the horses," Farmer Able said as he strode into the cow barn. He started for the first cow on the far end of the barn. Unfortunately, that cow was Clarice.

"My, my, my . . . trouble coming." The fretful cow could immediately see the potential danger as Farmer Able plodded up to her, his eyes bloodshot and head bruised. She felt a "four-stom-acher" coming on. That's what any cow calls a belch that ripples up through all four stomachs and fills the cud-chewer's mouth with the most gassy awfulness. For Clarice, who already had an acidy indigestion due to her mission to eat and chew less, a four-stom-acher had a particularly strong repugnance.

Yet despite her best bovine resolve, she couldn't help but have all manner of cow fidgetiness. (She refused to call it bull-headed-ness as she'd never consider herself on a level with Bob the bull, who was particularly thick.) She stood on a flat, concrete floor and had her head locked in a stanchion, for heaven's sakes. But that didn't stop her from hoof-rocking, which is what a nervous cow will always succumb to when uneasy.

Then it began. "Confounded cow! Stand still." Farmer Able bellowed, seeing her jittery dance. But she couldn't. As he washed down her utter and began to slap on the milker, Clarice continued to twitch.

"Here! Stop that!" the farmer yelled. He gave Clarice a quick slap. This only induced more fidgetiness. Up came the four-stom-acher. The nervous cow flinched from the gastro-assault, twisting her head around compulsively at the farmer. As she exhaled, the gassy fumes engulfed Farmer Able.

The good farmer turned nearly as green as the fumes issuing from Clarice's mouth. He fought to hold down the little bit of breakfast he'd eaten. What he did taste was putridness from his own sour stomach.

"You really mooooddled things up now," murmured Velma, the cow next to Clarice.

Clarice was alarmed as well. What was she thinking? She surely knew, *Whatever you do, don't make the man mad.* She braced herself for an even greater slap.

After the nasty belch, Clarice had snapped her head back around and was starring straight forward. There was no way she was going to face Farmer Able again. Another four-stomacher just might come up. But in the drawn-out moments that passed, no slap came. Clarice couldn't help herself. She slowly turned her head back around and looked at the farmer.

What she saw was quite perplexing. He just sat there on the one-legged stool. The milking machine was in place, doing its rhythmic in-and-out sucking. The farmer had done his job and presently the machine was doing its. No need for him to just sit there. But sit there he did.

Farmer Able appeared downright stupefied. And it wasn't the nausea that kept him. He simply sat staring at the machine that was doing just fine without his attention. The "fwit-fwoot, fwit-fwoot" sound coming from the pneumatic milker appeared to entrance him.

Clarice noticed that Velma had craned her head around to take a gander at the flummoxed farmer. This time she mooed nothing, but did catch Clarice's eye. Neither Velma nor Clarice could figure it out. After a moment, Velma simply rolled her big brown eyes, gave a little cow snort and went back to her feed.

What the cows didn't or rather couldn't begin to fathom were the goings-on in Farmer Able's mind—or rather in his deeper constitution. His small little world had been rocked by—of all things—wind and bugs. The farmer sat there on that milk stool, perched like a dumb turkey on a fence post. And though he appeared inactive, his thoughts were anything but.

It just couldn't be, he thought as he considered the cryptic phrase. It all was like a strange nightmare to him. *That's it. It was just some crazy dream. I knew I shouldn't have eaten that **I**-talian food*, the farmer reasoned, pronouncing the "I" like "eye." (Patience had cooked up the dish from a recipe in one of her lady magazines.) But somewhere inside he knew the memory was entirely unlike a dream and certainly not oregano induced.

For a moment he did reconsider the obvious: *He was just overworked and overstressed.* Any diligent farmer usually ignores this. After all, hard work is what you do. Those who complain are simply whiners or slackers.

The fact was, the farmer could not embrace what this really implied. He'd have to change the way he was doing things. If stress was indeed the problem, then surely he should find a better way to operate.

But was he ready to change things? No.

He would simply get busy. Yet he could not get away from that mysterious sentence: *It's not about me. It's not about me. It's not about me.* The words seemed to pulsate with the same rhythm of the milker, resonating ever louder with each repetition.

"Bah!" the farmer finally said out loud. This brought an immediate flinch from Clarice and a ripple of twitchy excitement down the whole row of cows. Again, however, fortunately for Clarice, it wasn't followed by a slap. No, the farmer issued a rebuke. Seeing that Clarice was not touching her feed, and once again mindful of the little book of numbers in his bib pocket, he yelled, "Why aren't you eatin' you dumb cow? Food makes milk. And your production is down."

Well moo-moo-to-you, Clarice thought. *The nerve of that guy.*

All this rattled around between Clarice's horns. However, with no opportunity for real communication, Clarice simply issued an agitated *harrumph* to herself. And then that nervous, twitchy mastication started in. She began to chew, chew, chew even though she was only chewing air.

Farmer Able noticed this incongruity. "What are you chewing on, you idiot cow! You're chewing on nothing."

Chew, chew, chew. Her nervousness continued. And her thoughts went right along with it. *I'm chewing nothing?! Ha!* Chew, chew, chew. *Look who's talking. You're chewing on nothing.* Chew, chew, chew. *And don't you think we don't see it!*

Again the farmer certainly heard none of this. He could not understand that his sour stomach—and sour outlook—had provoked hers. Anxiety certainly has a way of hijacking others. He finally shook his head, said "Ah heck!" and turned on his heel and walked away.

The rest of the day, Farmer Able came up with a litany of excuses meant to dismiss what had happened. But the more he tried to remove himself or rather remove that darned message— *It's not about me*—from his head, the more it remained. He couldn't get away from it and it wouldn't extract itself from him. Yes, it was ludicrous. The whole gosh darn phenomenon was as nutty as a Christmas fruitcake. But the resounding words were beginning to indicate that he, in fact, was the tough nut to crack.

The attitude and
behaviors
you lead with
will be followed.

11

Sunny's Sore

That evening, Farmer Able avoided going to his granary office. His ledger compulsion would just have to wait. The message that had blown in from the tree was the main reason he stayed away. He wasn't about to hear any of that again.

Farmer "Fix-it" had some repair work to do on the machinery. It was just the kind of mundane task that might becalm him. However, as he strolled toward the pole barn, he saw something that got his dander up. Sunny had forgotten to gather the eggs. She was about to leave to go to her play rehearsal, when father confronted daughter.

"Why are your eggs still in the henhouse?" he groused, emphasizing the *your* in the question.

"Dad, I don't have time right now. I'm late," she said as she started to get in the car.

"No. You need to do it now."

"You said I could do it later. Remember, we talked ..."

"You're not going off to some brainless play rehearsal when there's work to be done."

There it was. The farmer's true feelings about Sunny's extracurricular activity pierced her. But Sunny wasn't about to let him see the hurt. She rammed the car in gear and took off down the driveway.

Patience appeared, having heard them through the kitchen window. She and Farmer Able could only stand there and watch as the car hurled down the long driveway, spitting dust and stone.

Patience waited until Sunny was well away down the 318, then calmly said, "Honey, you did tell her she could wait 'til later on the eggs."

The farmer fumed. If he allowed himself to think about it, he might have just remembered that conversation about delaying the egg gathering. But he wasn't going to admit that. No, that was no longer the issue. His daughter's defiance was.

He just shook his head angrily and strode on to the pole barn.

He stayed out there until way after the sun had set. Turning wrenches did him some good. It rotated his mind away from his altercation with Sunny. More importantly, it relieved him of that haunting exhortation. Or so he thought. *Things are NOT "just about me,"* he cogitated. And the more he repeated it, the more he became convinced. He even bolstered his reasoning by thinking about how much he was sacrificing for his family . . . for Sunny, even though she was contrary . . . for the hired help . . . for the animals . . . heck for the entire farm! Indeed, he had put up with a lot, and it was entirely due to his *selflessness* that he had forfeited so much.

The more the wrenches turned, the tighter this justification became. By the time he had the planter fixed and the gears greased, he actually felt that his own thinking had been repaired and lubricated as well. He turned out the light in the pole barn and trudged home to bed, actually feeling like he could forget the whole, strange incident.

Alas, the unpredictable challenges of life have a way of underscoring things. The good and the bad come with curriculum attached. That very night, Farmer Able and Patience were awakened from sleep by a late night call. It was Lester Dettleman, two sections over. Sunny had driven into a pole on his property and wrecked the family car. Fortunately, other than a dislocated shoulder, Sunny was okay.

Farmer Able and Patience spent most of the night at the ER, listening to the wail of their daughter as the doctor put the joint back in place. Over the next few days, bruising emerged and with it a dull ache, but for the most part she was on the mend.

Patience played nursemaid, and even Farmer Able helped with adjusting her sling. He had to poke a few more holes in the straps to make her more comfortable. "Too tight?" he asked with a kindness Sunny hadn't seen for awhile.

By the third day, Sunny had made her way out into the yard to catch some sun. This was one of her favorite pastimes, she felt on account of her name. Her dad found her sitting in a chair, her face soaking in the sun.

Despite her obvious screw-up, the farmer hadn't been of a mind to bring up matters, considering her injury. He'd been waiting to address the issue of "responsible driving." He began the conversation taking the tack of sympathy. "Your shoulder feeling better?" he asked.

"Better, but pretty sore still."

"You just let it rest and heal. Won't be needing to use it for awhile."

"What's that mean?"

"I'm just saying you won't be using it for anything strenuous."

"Like chores?" Sunny meant it as a joke, but the hard-minded taskmaster didn't take it that way.

"For a time, but I figure you could be back at those in a week or so."

"A week?! That's ridiculous. I can't hardly lift a spoon, let alone feed animals."

"You don't need to get all huffy."

Harry the horse, who was in the side lot, couldn't help but listen in on this exchange. *Oh no*, he thought. *I wonder what the farmer whips her with?*

"Dad, I was just in a car wreck."

"*In* a car wreck . . . or *caused* a car wreck?" There it was. You could sense the laces on the gloves being untied.

"The county is doing construction out on the 318. They didn't mark it properly. It sprang up on me and I swerved."

"Sunny, you weren't paying attention. Don't deny it."

"My shoulder hurts. I don't need a lecture."

"I'm not lecturing. I'm telling you like it is. When that shoulder's back to working, there's going to be extra work for you. But you'll have the time. There's no way I'm giving you the keys back to go gallivanting around."

The clouds were mounting. "You know Dad," Sunny said. "You're right. It wasn't that the pylons were misplaced." Sunny had tears starting to well up. For a moment, Farmer Able thought he'd gotten through to his daughter. "I wasn't paying attention. But here's something you don't know. I was just following your lead."

"What?"

"I got mad just like you."

"What are you talking about?"

"You're always bellowin' around, slammin' doors when you can't handle things."

"Don't sass me."

"Just the opposite, Dad. I think you and I, now that I'm stuck here, will have more quality time together. Of course, I don't know why I think that would happen. You spend more time with the farm, the animals and those ledgers than you'd ever spend with me. You could say I'm not even equal to a horse, a cow or a chicken!"

"I have responsibilities," the farmer fumed.

"And obviously I'm not one of them." Then she blurted out, bursting into tears, "I got the lead in the play. Do you even know that? I guess it wouldn't matter. You weren't going to come anyway. You don't show up for me."

This caught Farmer Able off guard. His sobbing daughter suddenly reminded him of the little girl he remembered as a toddler who had bumped her knee.

Sunny's honesty continued to come in raw and unchecked. "It took a lot to get that role."

"That is ..." the farmer searched for the right word, "certainly somethin'."

"Somethin', huh?" Her ache came right up through her cynicism. "Somethin 'brainless,' right?"

The farmer's words came back at him like a dull echo.

Sunny wasn't finished. "Dad, what you said hurt so bad. I didn't know what to do. I just did what I see you doing when you have pains you can't handle. I got angry and lost control."

This final blow knocked the wind out of the good farmer. Sunny hurried into the house, her tears overwhelming her.

Later that evening, Harry the horse would tell the other animals about the whole incident, ending with, "... then he just stood there, saying nothing." There was a general, "serves him right" grumble that came up from most things hoofed and horned and certainly feathered. After all, the farmer "getting his comeuppance" was what most of the animals longed for. Yes sir, a thing whipped becomes a whipper indeed.

Of course, after they had let off this bit of steam, all the animals considered poor Sunny's plight. Despite his harsh treatment of them, the realization that the farmer had spent more time with the animals than his own daughter created a pang even in the hardest heart. For every creature knows the care of calf, colt and chick comes first in the universal order of things.

Sometimes,
a self-made man
can become
self-absorbed.

12

A Whistle at the Knothole

What the animals didn't see was that later that night Farmer Able made his way back toward his musty office. The ledgers beckoned. But after his daughter's rebuke, Farmer Able swore off that compulsion. He knew he had penciled in his work and worries too often. Now, he had quite another mission.

He didn't go to his desk but rather found himself out under the stars before the old walnut tree. It was a windless night. The quiet actually began to disturb the farmer. For a man steeped in perpetual clamor, this bit of silence was quite unnerving.

He was about to throw off the whole charade when a breeze came through. This didn't have the fierceness of the wind a few nights earlier. In this moment, it came like a lazy zephyr, enveloping him, rather than blowing at him. The ladybugs nearby always welcomed these gentle gusts; for them, flapping and fluttering weren't necessary. No, they could simply ride this kind of breeze like a sailboat.

The soothing wind had quite the unexpected effect of softening up the hard-crusted farmer. Oh, he'd felt the winds on innumerable occasions. Dust bowls, violent thunderstorms, grit blown in the eyes, dirt devils, the sideways sleet of a winter—he'd cursed them all. But this . . . why he was taken back to a moment in his youth when the warm breeze dried him under the sun after a swim at the lake.

"Pshaw!" he said out loud. Losing his wits was never something the farmer afforded himself. And his old work boots were tugging at him to turn and leave, given all this sentimental nonsense.

Then the wind's warmth embraced him again. He found he couldn't leave it. That old tree creaked a certain creak that bespoke a new phrase: *We* . . . tend . . . the . . . beans.

The farmer was perplexed. Was he hearing things right? Yes, these were English words wisping through the branches. But there was no real "mystery" in them. Being a farmer, of course he tended the beans. This sentence really meant nothing and actually made him feel the fool.

The breeze stopped. All was silent again. The farmer stood there for a while trying to make something of all this. But he was getting nothing, so he made his way back to his office.

The ants were there, continuing to march in their streaming lines. They were still after every crumb they could find, but he wasn't of a mind to get rid of them.

He opened his ledger book. It wasn't to mind his numbers. No, he looked down at the missive he'd jotted down earlier: *It's not about me.*

"Oh, I see what you're saying," the farmer said out loud as if talking to the wind. "'It's not about me' . . . really means . . . 'It's ALL about me.' I'm clear-headed now. You can answer me plain!"

Just then he heard the wind whistle at the knothole. In came the words he'd just heard, only he heard them more clearly: *We tend the **queen**.* Oh, not the ***beans**!*

Watching the ant parade, this clarification suddenly made sense. *Everybody knows there's the queen ant down in some nest somewhere, running things,* the farmer thought. *The workers do what the queen tells them. That means nothin' really, unless you're a servile ant . . .* or simply a person *who doesn't mind another telling him what to do.*

He still jotted the missive down in his ledger book. It kept rippling through the deeper recesses of the good farmer's soul.

"Bah!" he finally exclaimed.

These thoughts were quite onerous to the farmer. After all, at the root of it all, he'd gone into farming to be the captain of his fate. Oh, he was well aware of the volatility of the weather and grain prices. He definitely battled in a perpetual war with weeds and bugs. And he certainly understood there was a whole lot of gettin' your back under it. However, despite all the trials and tests, his prime reason for being was that Farmer Able was . . . his own man! He took pride in it—doing things his way.

Considering all this, something welled up inside the farmer and he proclaimed out loud to the ants, "Maybe slaving away, being a worker ant, serving some queen fits you fine. But I'm no ant." He put a particular edge on that last sentence, then he added with an outstretched wave of his hand, "All this around here, I made it myself. Everything is because of me. Everything that you see."

The words had no sooner left his mouth when a thought suddenly pierced the farmer. He remembered what his daughter had told him: *I was just following your lead.*

A thunderbolt—like the one he'd seen split an oak tree—struck him. He sucked in a breath, realizing just how wrong-headed he had been in the example he had set for Sunny. His audacity and pride had blinded him. In fact, all that he'd built, all that he'd made, the result of all his efforts . . . was a sham, in light of the way he had run roughshod over those he cared about most. In an effort to be a self-made man, he had become self-absorbed.

His derisive mocking of the worker ants for being little servants was quite hypocritical. For in his quest to rule over his little empire, to exert power and authority, to be the lord of his domain, he had in fact become a slave himself. He kowtowed to his obsession for number crunching, but worse, he was subservient to his craving for control. His own fear was his master and he bowed to it every day in a thousand ways.

He also realized something else. He imagined that stalwart queen somewhere down in her hidden nest. It could appear as if she was a bit of an egocentric tyrant, sending out all her drones to do her bidding. But Farmer Able pondered . . . at the heart of the ant monarch was one singular motivation: the very best interests of the entire nest. She absolutely could not even think or consider anything else. She was a self, spilling over with selflessness.

We tend the queen suddenly became not a constraining message of indentured servitude. No, it released a great freedom in this man shackled to his own compulsive anxiety.

Farmer Able actually felt himself longing to be like one of those carefree little ants, busy about their work, with a true eager purpose in mind. In their tiny ant heart of hearts he imagined they truly only had one purpose: to serve the rightful authority of the nest and in so doing serve the greater wellbeing of the entire colony itself.

Yes, it's true the farmer thought, the cobwebs of his deception dissolving away. *It truly is NOT about me.*

And in that instant, as this dawning broke like a broad country sky, a new message came whistling through the knothole: *Clean out the stalls.*

"Clean out the stalls," the farmer squinted. "What the heck!" Even though he was a man of simple understanding, he did consider it to be perhaps a farm metaphor of sorts. *I reckon I've got a lot of manure piles in my life that need cleaning out.*

But the message wasn't some highfalutin' puzzler. No, in the farmer's heart he knew it was what is was. He thought about the actual barn he'd let get out of control. He had been so busy focusing on "productivity"—plowing and planting—that he had let this awful job go. Now if you don't tend to a job like this for an entire winter, and the cows and horses keep consuming and expelling as any good cow and horse will do—well you can imagine how thick and rank things can really get.

The farmer could hardly get to sleep that night—not for worry, as was often the case— but because he couldn't wait to get at those mucky stalls. He ultimately did doze off. And sleep he did. He dozed so soundly that Ricardo the rooster had to crow especially hard—(with an extra dash of indignation, mind you)—until finally the sleeping farmer awoke.

Cleaning out
the stalls
is not
udderly ridiculous.

13

Putrid Perfumery

The filthy barn gave new meaning to the expression "piled high." The stalls were a mess, but mainly the shed. Here, the many eliminations hadn't been removed all winter. The animals had simply tramped it down to the point it was stuffed and overflowing.

Despite his enthusiasm, Farmer Able still couldn't help but let out a sigh—or rather hold back a wince—upon seeing and smelling the stinking heap. Yet that malodorous perfume permeated his hardened exterior like few things had been able to. For surely he had let many an awful thing "pile up." No matter how much he had tried to avoid the stench in his life, stink is still stink, and it doesn't just go away.

Normally, cleaning out the barn would be a task he'd assign to Ernie. That's what the hired help is for, right? They perform the jobs the boss doesn't want to. But Farmer Able was on a strange, wind-inspired mission.

Farmer Able cinched up his overalls and set about the arduous task. He had done this job a thousand times in his youth. Yes, this menial job was beneath him, but strangely, doing it offered the opportunity to elevate him above himself. He parked the manure spreader, grabbed a pitchfork and shovel and started in.

It wasn't long before Foreman Ryder saw (or rather heard from Ernie) what was going on. The exchange had gone like this:

"He's doin' what?"

"Cleaning out the shed."

"Well get on in there and help him."

"He won't let me. Wants to do it himself . . . or so he says."

This got Ryder's dander up. "Makes not a bit of sense," the foreman groused as he strode into the barn. Of course he quelled his temper once in the presence of his boss. "Ernie can do that," Ryder offered, with an air of firmness. The foreman had taken it as a personal affront that Farmer Able was bending a pitchfork. Ryder thought it made him look bad—like the farmer was rubbing it in his face. He even said, "I was fixin' to get to that job once the planting is done."

"Naw, I'll do it," was all Farmer Able said. "We'll get the planting done."

This was not an answer Foreman Ryder wanted to hear nor was it one he could understand. Not being a man who could tease out a deeper impetus, he spoke bluntly. "You don't need to get your boxers in a twist about it. If you don't like the way I'm managing things, just come out with it."

Farmer Able finally stopped forking and looked at Ryder. "I'm not upset with your work. I appreciate your efforts. This is just something I've got to do." How could the farmer say what had happened and what exactly was his motivation? No explaining in the world could enlighten Ryder regarding the wind's missive.

Ryder couldn't abide this answer, even though it was a compliment. He finally barked, "Confound it." He grabbed a pitchfork and started to help. "Don't understand why we're doing this when there's so many bloomin' other things more important to do."

Farmer Able could see plainly he'd upset his foreman. That was never his intent. He normally responded to surliness with his own form of vitriol. But on this morning, with a certain putrid perfumery softening his synapses, Farmer Able gave a more moderated reply. "You're right. There is much to be done elsewhere. Best you attend to it. I can handle this."

Because Ryder was always working the angles, he assumed everyone else was as well. He paused and crooked a dubious eye. His wheels were churning in great disarray. *What was the blasted farmer up to?* In Ryder's world, he was far better at contending with dust-ups and dress-downs. Those he could understand. But this?

"Go on," Farmer Able urged. "Go on and get to the planting. That would be good."

"Suit yourself," Ryder said. He stabbed his pitchfork into the mound like a combatant conceding his sword. *This is gonna come back on you. Yes sir*, he thought. Then he strode away, yelling for poor Ernie.

Farmer Able certainly felt the full weight of this exchange. It was entirely foreign to him and yet at the same time utterly freeing. He hadn't given Ryder a "what for." He only knew he was somehow right without making sure everyone knew he was in the right. That release brought something he hadn't known for some time: a smile.

And there in the stink-infested shed, an inner fragrance of sorts had wafted up in his subconscious: the scent of goodness. There was a down-to-earth virtue in this—a newfound freedom with every forkful.

What he didn't realize was that unlike Ryder's response, the hoofs and horns had an entirely different reaction. It had taken no longer than the flutter of a hummingbird's wing for the news of Farmer Able's task to spread down through the back barn lot and pasture.

"Did you hear? Did you see?" young Bridgette said, trotting up to the herd. The cows— curious by nature—left their grazing and hurried to the barn upon hearing the news. Cows don't have those large, doleful eyes for nothing. Yes, they're for spying out the best grazing spots to be sure, but it's a little known secret they're also for focused gazing—and none more than Clarice.

Just when she thought she might be ready to give up her cud-chewing disorder, she found this news to be a new worry. She hurried with the rest of them, their tales swishing and udders wagging in opposing directions. Many a Jersey in that cantering herd issued cow curses under their breath, mooing, "If that Bridgette has mislead us, why ..." The sentences weren't finished because frankly a cow on the run is plumb out of breath.

But Bridgette's report was confirmed when they saw first the manure spreader and then, to their great shock: Farmer Able on the working end of a pitchfork. "My, my, my," Velma could only say, gasping to catch her breath. Other cow expressions pierced the morning air, including "Udderly ridiculous!" and "This is a bigger leap than a cow jumping over the moon." Most just said—at least this is what the farmer and any other human could hear— "Moo. Moo. Moooo," which is about as emphatic as anything a cow might articulate.

Bob the bull sauntered up as well. He was normally aloof (thinking this was the best approach to endear himself to a herd of heifers), but now he couldn't help himself and said, "What's his beef?"

Harry the horse and his friends trotted up to gawk as well. Jay couldn't believe it and decided to stick his nose in the barn door, snorting and sniffing to get the full experience. "Better watch it," Harry said. "You'll get a swift crack on that nose." Farmer Able came up to Jay, which did give him a start. But the farmer's outstretched hand wasn't bringing a slap. No, he actually petted Jay's blazed face.

"There, boy," Farmer Able said. "Pretty soon, when you go to sleep at night, it'll be in fresh straw."

The words "fresh straw" were flabbergasting. All things furry wished at that moment they didn't have hoofs so they could stick a finger in their ears and swab them out. Were they really hearing this?

"Yes sir," Farmer Able said getting back to his forking, "out with the rotten and in with the forgotten." (Farmer Able's grandpa had always said this, but only now did it register.)

"Doesn't make a lot of horse sense," Harry neigh-sayed. And many of the cows were quick to agree. "He's got something up those overalls." The cows were all still smarting under the reduced rations Farmer Able had imposed. To say these cows had become dubious was an understatement.

"Well," Velma smirked, "even if the hose of kindness gets unkinked, the outflow might just be a soaking, not a true watering."

"We cows certainly know what it means to have a thick hide," Velma mooed. "You'd think that hard-fisted farmer of all people would know that." There was a general chorus of moos in agreement with this insight. "He's not going to fool us with this charade of niceness. He's up to something."

Strangely, Clarice, who had been taking all this in, was quiet. She didn't moo approval or disapproval. She just listened and watched as the farmer continued to fill the spreader. Sweat formed on his brow. Clarice focused on this. Actually she narrowed those big brown eyes on the very bruised spot that still remained from his goose egg. This injury was of particular note, for oddly it symbolized the farmer's peculiar behavior.

What had gotten into Farmer Able? Had he fallen and been

knocked silly? This didn't seem to follow any train of logic. No, perhaps he actually had some sense knocked into him. But by whom?

There was something in the air that Clarice couldn't wrap her horns around. And then she noticed: her compulsive, worried, resentful cud-chewing had ceased. Oh, this scene before her was a conundrum indeed. But strangely, it becalmed not bothered her. For the first time in weeks, she didn't grind away at her tongue and teeth. No, the "out with the rotten, in with the forgotten" brought a general spark of possibility that even a worried cow could understand. Or so it seemed.

The only thing she could do, the only thing left to do, was to get back out to the pasture and cogitate on this. Mastication or no mastication, she was going to understand what the farmer was up to.

Self-reflection
is illuminating.

14

The Mud Puddle

Over the next several days, Farmer Able continued to clean out the shed. He tried to keep his mind focused on his new thoughts. However, the good farmer responded like so many when challenged by change: he began to wonder if this whole *clean out the stall* thing was really such a good idea.

To make matters worse, the tyranny of the urgent kept distracting him. The shining light of the way things could be, seemed to be confounded by the pressing concerns of the way they'd always been. Those old work routines and habits appeared to offer such comfort, even though that oldness had not worked. He also found himself compulsively wanting to check the little ledger in his pocket.

So given all this, when justifiable reasons came up to quit the stall cleaning, he took them. For instance, Ernie and Ryder needed a disk to further break up the fields. The disk was stored at an old shack down the lane on the back forty. This ramshackle place still had just enough roof to keep most of the weather out and thus was used to keep any implement that the overstuffed pole barn couldn't hold.

Ernie offered to go get the disk. But Farmer Able knew there was still much to be planted, and he didn't want to take Ernie off the job. "I'll bring it to you," Farmer Able said. So he stopped his stall cleaning, unhitched the horses from the manure spreader and took the team down the lane to retrieve the implement.

Chester, one of the older horses in this team, saw immediately what was going on. "Yep," the horse said. "The man thinks he's all about cleaning out our stalls. But that was just horse feathers. We horses know where these hoofs stand on his list of priorities."

Chester certainly didn't need Harry's neigh-saying to know a showy sham when he saw one. "It's just like the humans to think they can put one over on us 'dumb' animals," he snorted.

Farmer Able and the team reached the old shed, which was a good half mile down the lane. He started to hitch up the disk when the black clouds of a large thunderstorm rolled in. Soon there was a downpour. Farmer Able tied up the horses under an eave, and he ducked in the shed to wait out the storm.

"No use getting drenched trying to get back to the barn lot. It'll pass soon," the farmer said. He actually issued this with a grumble, because a man of action isn't real happy about being confined when there's work to be done.

He found an old crate and sat down. He stared out at the rain. It took awhile to settle himself. After all, this "break" was not scheduled. But nature pouring down on itself is a mesmerizing thing. There was something about the skies opening and the fields receiving that slowed him down. Being busy meant he could be distracted and not think about things. But darn it, if that rain wasn't keeping him from being preoccupied. Even now as he stared out, he looked inward.

Despite the fresh washing of sky and earth, the grimy turmoil of his life weighed heavily—especially Sunny's recent accident. Avoiding the issues encircling him wasn't really an option.

As he sat there, a puddle formed, just out from the eave. He wasn't sure what compelled him, but he stood up and walked over to it. Sure enough, he could see himself. He thought, *who is this man?* He wasn't just considering the haggard, whisker-stubbled face that stared back at him. No, the person in his inquiry lived somewhere behind that worn-out visage.

That man had been challenged sure enough by a silly thing like the whispering wind. He felt a simple call to make some changes. But had he? Or more importantly, was he willing to?

Hard questions seemed to resonate as he stared at the silent image in the puddle. *How can I improve? What changes need to be made? Is what I'm doing truly working or is there a better way?*

His first inclination was to always think about the farm and his work. But now the circle extended further out to his family. *Am I taking care of them?* This self-inquiry wasn't just about bread on the table. He had always provided that 'a plenty. No, at this juncture, the cacophony of Patience's kind admonitions and Sunny's unchecked but certainly honest anger seemed to rise up from that puddle reflection as well. And perhaps for the first time he didn't deflect to, *well that's their problem.* No, he considered, *what's my role in all of this?*

Farmer Able remembered old man Guthrie telling him once, as he rocked in his chair on his porch, "A question stretches things; a statement shrinks things." This little riddle that Farmer Able didn't really understand at the time was becoming clear. *Yep, a good question is certainly better than a simple statement.* He could see that the "ask" of a question can pierce through the well-thought out, but often limited, hard-and-fast statements we live by.

At this moment, Farmer Able was caught up in the "ask" of all these questions. The very possibilities of the many answers were indeed stretching him. His mind, which had desperately hung on to old ways, was loosening its grip. How, in the light of all that had happened, could he continue to do what he had been doing?

Even as the rain washed the sky, Farmer Able felt his way of doing things being washed away. There was something better. He could make changes. He certainly didn't like the worn-down guy in the puddle. He saw that he could shed all this heavy load of stress, this confounded way of doing things, this hammer and anvil rigidity.

Yes, I reckon I could change.

He had realized the hard questions, which he had many times avoided, weren't so hard anymore. They actually had pried open his spirit and he could see a new way of doing things. Change suddenly became not a burdensome idea, but a possibility to be embraced. Taking care of those around him, especially his family, didn't have to be a chore but a blessing. Truly caring was truly liberating. He didn't have to hold onto his world so tightly and push away those he loved.

As Farmer Able stood there watching the thunderclouds move off into the distance and the rain slowly abate, he felt washed just like the earth before him.

He was going to attempt to make things right with Sunny. Just how, he wasn't sure. But he knew he'd find a way.

Chester knew nothing of this little mud puddle encounter. However, Farmer Able was also thinking about the horses, even though the horses didn't know he was. His cleaning out the stalls was indeed a good thing. Why compromise? Go the whole way with it.

When the rain finally stopped, Farmer Able hitched the team to the disk. They made their way back up the lane to the barnyard. As he went, the sun peeked back through the clouds and sure enough a rainbow arched its way across the sky. Somewhere in that place just past his whiskered face, those colors registered with the farmer. That grand spectacle of hue and luster was actually nothing more than an outward display of his inner brightness. The bowing colors against gray sky were exactly how he felt at that moment. They offered an abiding hope. Yes, he could change. Yes, he could improve. Yes, he did care.

Out with
the rotten,
in with
the forgotten.

15

Days of Straw and Sawdust

It actually wasn't Farmer Able's intent to make some impression on the animals. No, he simply was charged by a new impulse. He went back to cleaning out the shed with a new vigor. With each forkful there was a subtle repetition of the idea: *out with the rotten, in with the forgotten.* And the result of this was a constitution reworked.

To him it felt like the time he'd put drainage tile in a field so the marshes wouldn't keep flooding out the crops. The swampy water in his thinking was being drawn off, making the soil good for growing.

He worked for several more days cleaning out the shed. He took load after load out to the fields and spread it. He finally had rediscovered the actual floor of the barn. Once it was completely cleared, he then covered it with fresh straw and fluffy sawdust. His muscles ached from all the heave-hoing. But it was a good burn—for as anyone knows, exhaustion from an honorable effort always is its own reward.

Finally, Farmer Able let the animals in with an air of expectation. But not everyone shared his enthusiasm.

This was such a curious sight to Harry the horse and his friends that they paused at the doorway, again snorting and sniffing before entering. Harry had borne many of Farmer Able's angry oaths and whip cracks. He wondered what strange inducement this was. "This isn't all molasses and oats," Harry nickered dubiously. "Just wait 'til tomorrow. That rawhide lash will come out again. No amount of sugar's going to change that," he whinnied.

Louis the cat, who was a bit of a jester, noticed Harry's neigh-saying. He couldn't help but comment: "Even if you give some horses clover, they're still not going to lie down in it."

Harry was offended, first because as a fine, strong horse he didn't lie down for anything or anybody, and second because he didn't like smart-mouthed cats. Louis scurried away adding an extra barb, "You're stubborn as a mule." Harry nearly snapped his halter trying to get at the cat. Everyone knows the greatest offense to a horse is to be compared to their half-breed, half-witted relatives.

Jay, on the other hand, was glad because the straw and sawdust gave his flat, dry hoofs a tickle. He was also happy that the olfactory rancor of all that cow dung was gone. (The cows had the same response to the absent horse manure. A creature never thinks their muck is as bad as another's.) Even cantankerous Chester finally saw that Farmer Able's effort wasn't just all show. The farmer had actually come through on his promise.

However, a few of the cows had a peculiar reaction to the clean barn. Some even complained that the "deep warmth" of the former manure pile they had slept on all winter was nicer. They actually hinted that they missed it. They sure wanted Farmer Able to hear it from the herd. Their moos became a veritable cow chorus.

One cow thought the farmer did it so he wouldn't have to

spend so much time washing dirty udders before milking. It was a bit of bovine bluster, suggesting the farmer was lazy.

Another bovine, who had a head for numbers, calculated that this extra expense of hay and sawdust meant even tighter rations on their feed was coming. "You watch," she mooed. "I'll bet a salt lick he'll reduce our stingy three-quarter scooper full to half when he's parceling out the feed tomorrow morning."

"To be certain," Velma intoned, "things oughta stay as they are." Velma said this even as she nestled down in the straw. Yes, you give cows enough time to masticate on a change and all manner of rationales will emerge. She added with a sniff, "Yep, Farmer Able made his bed . . ."

But before she could get out the end of that sentence, Louis finished the thought: ". . . and now *you* get to sleep in it." The cat chuckled to himself as he skipped up to the haymow.

Velma was upset. She liked to think no good Jersey ever took offense. After all, when it comes to Jerseys—who pride themselves on having the richest butterfat content of any cow—the cream certainly always rises to the top. But ego has a way of deceiving even a cow.

Clarice was still quite dismayed. She listened to all the mooing and moaning. It was her general disposition as a proud member of the herd to pitch in with her own grumbling and grievances. But something compelled her to hesitate. There was just something about the freshness of that straw.

Farmer Able didn't hang around to notice all this. Nor would he have understood the many cow considerations ahoof. There was a spark—a candle of possibility—flickering between the two horns on Clarice's head. Could it be that a little dung removal might actually lead to an attitude adjustment? Perhaps it was too early to tell.

All Clarice knew was that night she dreamed of straw being spun into gold.

Truly caring
allows you
to carry 50 times
your weight.

16

That Old Whip

Farmer Able continued to shore up the many forgotten things around the barn—fixing this and cleaning out that. Why, he even trimmed the horses' hoofs, which will make any steed feel light-footed and even a bit light-hearted.

Perhaps all this effort was due to shame. Even when Farmer Able's heart was cold and his head so calculating, he knew deep down he was mistreating his furry friends. He began to see that whipping them into shape had actually been born of whipping himself inside.

Certainly this Old Dirt knows the real grit that can sully a human heart. Shame has a certain escalating cycle. The more people feel bad, the more they pursue bad; the more they pursue bad, the more they feel bad. That's the mucky-muck of it.

Strangely, it was the wind that had given Farmer Able a reprieve. The message, though at first quite an offense, was liberating. The farmer's self-destructive road to perdition had certainly earned him a just punishment. You sow to the wind; you reap the whirlwind. But here was the wind offering just the opposite: a clean breath of fresh air. The initial message *It's not about me*—once grasped—had actually elevated the farmer to a position outside of himself.

Could it be that somewhere where the wind originated—perhaps resonating in the greater ether of the universe—love had trumped the hate in the farmer's heart? Maybe this was the joy the farmer was now feeling, like a prisoner released from irons.

An unexpected transformation also alighted. Farmer Able's fear was replaced by a general sense of compassion. The farmer remembered a fact he'd learned about ants some time ago. Though they may be tiny, they can carry 50 times their body weight. He thought, as he considered their self-sacrificing ethic: maybe their earnest hearts have the capacity of 50 x 50 when it comes to caring.

Farmer Able figured the tracks they made across his ledger book pointed to a new way of thinking. The panic that had compulsively caused him to pencil in those ever-dwindling numbers could now be erased. That's not to say productivity and profits were to be ignored. No, all these new ideals would be his approach to creating higher yields.

As his own self-flagellation abated, he became more aware of his lashing out at others. Amends needed to be made. He put away the whip and the dreaded twitch he'd used on Harry and the other horses. He considered Ernie's gentle hide stroking in the milk barn and tried to emulate it. Strangely, coaxing out the milk was a concept that resonated. Yes, this new approach was largely unfamiliar, but in the deeper recesses of his newly formed being, it all added up.

Beware

the little foxes.

17

Sparky

Farmer Able had many opportunities to put his new ideas into practice. One day he stopped by a farm that had fallen on hard times. Farmer Bitterman was liquidating and moving to town. Farmer Able didn't buy any equipment, but he did discover the farmer had a dog, named Sparky, who needed a new home.

"He's quite the herder," Bitterman boasted. "He can bring in anything on four hoofs. Can't you boy?"

Sparky was one happy dog. "*Yap! Yap!*" Sparky's ears perked, eyes widened and tail wagged at the mere thought of rounding up livestock.

Farmer Able took an immediate liking to him. He thought Sparky would be a good dog to have around. After all, every farm needs a barker and a herder.

He put him to work right away. "You ready to bring up the cows and horses?" Farmer Able asked.

Sparky barked excitedly. Oh, did he understand this. *Yap! Yap!* might as well have been *Yes! Yes!*

At the farmer's command, Sparky took off. He weaved and circled, expertly gathering the horses and cows. He brought them right up into the back barn lot.

"Why, if that isn't the darndest thing," Farmer Able said, petting the dog when he returned. "Good boy." And Sparky wagged his tail in agreement.

Sparky was so good at his task and so trusted that—heck—all Farmer Able had to do was whistle and off he would go. Farmer Able could then tend to other things while the dog brought up the herd.

But Sparky was a wily dog. As soon as he saw that the farmer wasn't watching, he didn't care to bring the herd in slowly and patiently. *Why do that?* he thought. *My job is to move them from pasture to barn lot. As long as that happens, what does the farmer care how it's done?*

So when the farmer's back was turned, he went after the herds, nipping and biting at their heels.

"You dreaded mutt," Clarice would bellow as Sparky pushed her to a full cow canter. "Can't you see I'm hurrying here?"

"You want our milk churned to butter before we even get to the barn?" Velma mooed.

Harry and the other horses would kick up their heels at the dog. "If I could just land one hoof on that mongrel," Harry groused. But Sparky was cagey and always managed to avoid every hoof.

Sparky loved teasing the herds just to see them get upset. "You fat, old lazy cows," Sparky woofed. "If you would just do what the farmer wants and not linger down here gorging yourself on clover then I wouldn't have to bite."

"Why, I never," Clarice mooed. "Doesn't that flea-bitten mutt even notice that with my nervous stomach I've sworn off clover?" She could feel her cud-chewing disorder returning, and she slowed up just to spite that dog.

But the sneaky Sparky didn't respond directly to Clarice's complaint. No, he nipped at Velma's heels. "What are you bitin' at me for, you mongrel?" Velma mooed. "I'm moving out." Then Velma got mad at Clarice. "Get goin' you loafer. Start hoofin' it."

"Hey, I'm not the problem. It's the mutt."

And on and on the cows quarreled, turning on each other for not high-stepping it.

Sparky howled with delight over all this. Oh, how he liked to stir the proverbial pot. Why he'd even turn horse against cow, biting at the equines if the cows were slow and biting at the bovines if the horses were plodding. Harry got so agitated he would even reach over and bite Clarice on the rump to hurry up.

For Sparky, this was just too much dog-eat-dog fun. "Bunch of grass-gobblers," he barked, adding further insult to injury. "Who says you can't turn vegetarians into meat eaters?" That remark would certainly harangue any herbivore.

This went on for a while without Farmer Able noticing. After all, the herds came up from the field and he didn't have to do anything but whistle.

But then the farmer began to observe that the livestock arrived not only out of breath, but also out of sorts. It took awhile to get Harry and the horses to settle down just to get their harnesses on. And the cows were so jittery and jumpy, they often wouldn't relax to eat their feed and let down their milk.

When Farmer Able would watch Sparky bring up the herds, the same patient weaving and gathering took place. But what the farmer didn't hear was, "Go ahead. Bite me, you mangy mutt," Clarice mooed. "Show the farmer what you're really all about."

Sparky was always such a "good dog" in front of the farmer. In fact, when Farmer Able spoke to the dog, all he ever got was the same enthusiastic *Yap! Yap! Yes! Yes!*

The farmer remained perplexed until one day after he had whistled for Sparky to bring up the herds. The wind kicked up and whispered, *Beware the little foxes.* This whoosh of insight blew the wool off the farmer's eyes.

He pretended to go in the barn. But he actually circled around and peeked out the back doorway. To his horror, he watched Sparky nip and bite, running the herds at full gallop.

"Well I'll be doggone," Farmer Able fumed. Sparky was not doing doggy tricks but was full of foxy trickery.

This would have normally sent the farmer into a rage. But inspired by his new wind-driven approach to things, Farmer Able thought he could breathe new life into Sparky.

Over the next several weeks, Farmer Able patiently tried everything to encourage Sparky to change. He gave positive pats and firm noes. He would keep him on a short leash if he didn't respond and offer him meaty bits from his own table if he did.

But no matter how many inducements, Sparky always responded the same way: *Yap. Yap. Yes. Yes.* And when the farmer wasn't looking, he went right back to his old ways. Farmer Able came to realize that behind that wide-eyed eagerness was nothing more than dogged narrow-mindedness.

Things actually got worse. The farmer noticed that some of the animals were coming in with blood on their back legs. Sparky was biting at the wellbeing of the whole herd. Man's best friend had become Farmer Able's worst nightmare.

The farmer had no choice. He found a new home for Sparky— at a junkyard where he could nip at the heels of all the trash he wanted.

(Later, Farmer Able heard that Bitterman had actually promoted this nip-and-bite technique. Farmer Able wondered: *Did Bitterman's farm fall on hard times because his harsh methods had finally caught up to him?*)

SPARKY

The hoofs and horns were certainly grateful for Sparky's dismissal. "Sometimes you can't teach an old dog new tricks," Clarice and the others commiserated.

Louis the cat, who certainly had no love lost for Sparky, quipped, "but you can certainly teach an old farmer a new fix."

Help someone else
grow
and everyone
grows.

18

Growing Pains

Despite this setback, Farmer Able still believed his newfound approach would be quickly embraced and adopted. But change isn't easy. The ripple of discontent had already started with Foreman Ryder. Over the next few days, that creek persisted to rise.

"Me and Ernie can only plant what's been plowed and disked," Ryder said to Farmer Able when he came in from the field. The arrangement all spring had been one plowed the field, one disked it and one planted it. But now Farmer Able was off on what Ryder referred to as "a hare-brained goose chase." (Ernie heard the mixed metaphor in this, but wisely chose not to point it out to Ryder.)

In Ryder's mind, the readying and planting were falling behind. He had berated Ernie to stay on top of things, micromanaging every moment of his time. But there was only so much back-and-forth in the fields, in any one man, on any given day—and Ryder knew it.

"We're already working sun up to sun down," Ryder complained to Farmer Able. "At this rate, there's acreage not going to get planted in time. And the crops won't be mature before the autumn frost. You do the math."

Farmer Able had to smile at this expression: *You do the math.*

He realized that in the past several weeks since the wind and ants had showed up, he hadn't pulled out his little numbers book in his overalls nor had he penciled in any figures in his office ledger.

Confident he was on the right course, he told Ryder, "You don't need to stress over this. The numbers will take care of themselves. I think what we're doing here will pay off." Farmer Able tried to explain his new purpose. "When you help something else grow, everything grows, including yourself. We're talking about the greatest good for all."

"So now the cows and horses are running things?" Ryder groused.

One could almost see the steam coming out the ears of the git-'er-done foreman. He was certainly of no mind to attend to the needs of the hoofs and horns beneath him. After all, they were animals—simply objects to be manhandled.

And though he'd never admit it, that same authoritative mindset extended to the one above him as well. He liked to think he was actually in charge of the one who was in charge of him. He knew how to accomplish all these tasks better than the boss!

But now Ryder had a real problem, because what the boss was asking for wasn't a task at all. No, this method was a mindset. Farmer Able was simply encouraging Ryder to keep up his good work and the farmer would continue his.

As Ryder watched the farmer clean up the barns and take a hankering to the animals' wellbeing, he came to despise the beasts even more. For him it came down to "deserving" a thing, and those animals hadn't "deserved" anything—especially given their falling production numbers, which Ryder was well aware of.

This stuck in his craw, because Ryder had quite the elevated sense of fairness. Never mind that he didn't see things hypocritical in his own behavior. No, his own shortcomings were easily swept under the rug. Justified and excused—such was the Ryder high court ruling regarding himself—but woe to another if his twisted sense of right was breeched. As far as he saw things, everybody and everything never quite met his standards—leastways the lowly beasts.

With Farmer Able's newfangled approach, Ryder actually became even more entrenched. In light of the kindness the farmer was showing the animals, Ryder actually ratcheted up his tyranny. He was determined to power through. They "deserved" a swift kick, an extra tug, a yank away from the water trough even when they weren't done drinking.

The conclusion that infused the herd was simply this: Farmer Able is to blame. One would have to backtrack just a little to understand the cow logic operating here. The herd was already suspicious of Farmer Able's newfound niceness. They were all just waiting for the other hoof to drop. (A cow, being a quadruped, imagines not just one more hoof could drop, but an additional three. This certainly makes clear the breadth of cow cynicism.)

And drop it did, in the form of Ryder unloading on them. But did these bodacious bovines place the proper blame on Ryder? No. They considered themselves keener than this. They attributed the fault to Farmer Able. They didn't trust all these changes.

Some of the cows were more certain than ever that having the shed back with its "deep warmth" would be far better. Harry the horse, after getting stung by an especially hard whack from Ryder, cynically concluded that Farmer Able had trimmed his hoofs to get more work out of him. Yes, he could see the true motivation. That kindness was all horse feathers indeed.

The chorus of woe actually grew in spite of Farmer Able's new approach. Oh, how they longed for "the good old days."

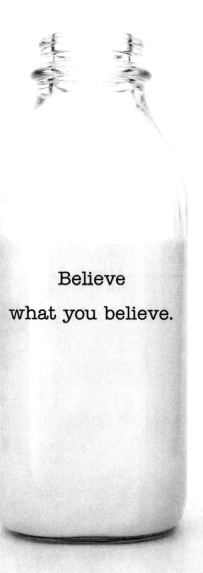

Believe
what you believe.

19

Embraced by the Wind

Farmer Able could feel the pushback from the hoofs, horns and hands all around him. Though he wasn't overtly tallying it, he knew milk production still wasn't up. The fields weren't getting planted. And general morale was still down. Despite his positivity, the farm didn't appear to be buying what he was selling.

He figured that maybe the herds were still reeling from all the years of abuse. Also, despite getting rid of Sparky, he thought the cows might just have a residual jitteriness that would take a while to overcome.

The farmer attempted to reassure himself and remain buoyant. But he knew that any tender shoot of change is always the most vulnerable, so he was worried this new plan might just wilt away. The good farmer grew anxious.

He plopped down in his office chair one evening and found himself compulsively wanting to pencil in those declining numbers—as if that would change things!

Unimagined by the farmer, these quivers in his heart actually made their way out to the wind. For if the wind is anything, it is keenly aware of a human heart's fluttering.

The knothole was a two-way corridor. Out went the farmer's

fears and within only a few breaths, in came the swirling wind. It whistled through the knothole with new wind words, starting with: *Believe…*

The farmer was, or at least had tried to be, on board with this high-minded idea. But "shame" rattled his keys again as Farmer Able realized he was actually faltering in the "believe" category.

The wind gathered itself and finished its refrain: *Believe what you believe.*

At first this was a puzzler. To Farmer Able, it seemed a bit redundant as in, "Of course I believe what I believe; otherwise I wouldn't believe it." But then he chewed on the deeper meaning. *What do I believe . . .* really?

As he pondered this, he looked over on the wall. He had hung a few framed photographs. There was Patience and Sunny, of course. In the center of this grouping was one of those aerial shots of his farm. His family farm had come down to him from his father's mother's father. It wasn't just land and lapboard buildings. No, it was . . . well . . . him. He "believed" in all it stood for.

It suddenly dawned on him. He was terrified of losing it. If he lost the farm, he wouldn't just lose a home and the security that came with it. No, he'd lose himself altogether. He would be a loser. A failure.

Just then he wondered: *Had he believed only in what he feared?* Had fear been driving him all these years? Is this why he was so rough on himself and everything around him? He had to make sure come heck or high water that the farm wouldn't go under—that he wouldn't go under.

As these questions wafted through his head, the wind gusted again. Farmer Able heard the little singsong in the knothole. He was reminded that the creak of the wind had irritated him before. But now he found himself actually yearning for it.

He sprang from his chair and flung open the old granary window. *Whoosh!* came the wind. He shut his eyes and threw back his head, letting it rush over him like a cavalcade. Ahh, the vitality of the spring breeze as it brought up the newness of the freshly planted fields was like music to his ears.

Farmer Able looked back as he stood there in the breeze: *What's there to fear? I'm a unique person in the world. I have something to offer. I'm embraced by the wind itself. And because of that sense of belonging to something beyond myself, I can inspire others with their own self-worth. Yes, that is what I believe.*

That evening, the wind carried away his shadows. In this new light, Farmer Able saw one thing he clearly had to do. He looked over at the photographs of Patience and Sunny. He had always justified his bad behavior, thinking, *I'm doing all this for them.* But that dusky excuse just had to go. He knew he had to set things right.

There's a
wonder and magic
in leaving your
ego behind
and
serving others.

20

Bubbles and Dishrags

To say "I'm sorry" is never easy—unless the ears hearing are Patience herself. For as mentioned, this woman was all about waiting for the thing unseen to be finally seen. And now here he came, up from his musty office in which he usually barricaded himself.

The apology that followed was simple and true. Farmer Able went one step further than mere words themselves. He did something he'd never done before: help with the dishes. That task was always, in his mind, hers . . . or rather, to be honest, "beneath him." But there was a new froth and sparkle to this humdrum job. The two pioneers, who had tilled the ground together and knew the sweat of hard labor, found a joy long forgotten in this scrubby little chore.

Farmer Able finally realized all this happiness had nothing to do with the task the hands were accomplishing. No, the heart was where this connection was made. And talk about power. For is there anything more potent than the pulse of two engaging as one—over bubbles and dishrags no less?

The clean dishes were finally all neatly stacked, but a certain mess remained. Farmer Able had to address his failures with Sunny.

She was up in her room. They hadn't really talked since their most recent argument. Farmer Able's pride—or rather embarrassment—couldn't abide it. But that drained away like so much dirty sink water.

His knock was met with a terse, "What do you want?" She had heard his heavy steps coming down the hall.

"Can we talk?" he said through the locked door.

"I think you've said your piece." That phrase had a particular barb because Farmer Able had often used it on her. Now he was getting that same brushoff from his daughter. This particularly smarted, because once again he was reminded that he had patterned her bad behaviors.

"I know I've said too much. And for that I'm sorry."

Only silence came through the door.

In the past, the farmer would have thought, *Well I've done all I can. It's up to her.* But there was no washing his hands of it.

In the silence that was filling the hallway, he discovered something. Silence was always something he had avoided. Silence meant facing yourself and your failures. But now that same stillness was welcomed. Yeah, that was it. Before, silence had been a clanging gong reminding him of all that he wasn't. However, that clamor was gone. He actually felt, for the first time, through the very closed door before him, the pain within his daughter's heart.

He had no sooner thought this than he left her door and hurried outside.

Sunny heard him leave and thought *good riddance!* But that reaction was mixed. She was happy he wasn't bugging her, but she remained angry thinking he didn't truly care or he would have stayed. Yet she barely had time to reflect on this when she heard his voice again outside her door.

"Sunny," Farmer Able said, "I got something for you. Well, actually it's for me."

Sunny always hated her dad's dumb riddles. What was her pathetic father up to?

"Could you just, please, open the door?" he asked with a softness she had rarely heard.

"Just go, dad."

But he wasn't leaving.

Then she saw something unexpected. A thin line of blue paper came from under the door. Sunny wasn't sure what it was at first. But then she saw clearly. It was a long strip of perforated tickets. It just kept coming.

They were tickets to her play.

"Dad, what are you doing?"

"I bought 'em. I want to go to your play."

Again silence came from behind the door.

"It's not every day your daughter gets the lead. So I bought extra, because I want to invite all of our friends to go, too."

After a long pause, Sunny finally opened the door. Her dad entered.

"I'm sorry, honey," the farmer said. "I really am. I realize I've been so worried about how the farm is doing, I forgot about you."

He stood there in his work-worn overalls. Yes, the days and years of toil were still imprinted, but now there was honesty to it all. Sunny could feel it. It was as if the fissure that had opened up within the broken farmer allowed him to access a tenderness she hadn't seen for a while. Out it came. "Nothing you do will ever change how much I love you."

Sunny couldn't help but screw up her face at this remark. "Dad, the car was almost totaled." She knew her father always evaluated things based on their cost.

But he headed off her thoughts. "You mean more to me than

the car. I don't care about the expense. I'm sorry I put my work ahead of you. I know I haven't been there for you."

Sunny could see the earnestness in her father's face. She could feel that she wasn't just a debit in his ledger column. He was willing to lavish true riches on her that had nothing to do with money.

"I forgive you," she said. "And I'm sorry for what I did."

The bear of a man who had wrestled with storms and droughts, dust and thistles now lovingly hugged his daughter. The tempest in her life began to roll away, leaving a fresh-washed calm behind.

Over the days and weeks to come, things continued to blossom within his family. Farmer Able kept getting more "windy" little inspirations. He set his heavy ledgers aside, but still took up his pencil. This time, however, he wrote two handwritten notes: one to Patience and one to Sunny. The farmer never fancied himself a man of deep expression, but something very down-to-earth was stirring in his heart. He wrote with a simple honesty what Patience and Sunny meant to him. He thanked them for their tolerance, their forgiveness and above all their many kindnesses. Needless to say, these weren't mere words. No, as the two women read them, they evoked the sweetest refrain, a kind of music that plays in the soul.

Farmer Able and Patience did go to see Sunny in the play. When they were about to leave that evening, he did a simple thing, a gesture that had an unspeakable grandness. "You can drive," he said to his daughter. As she drove them, her hands steady on the wheel, Farmer Able was content that a bit of that fragrant wind had been passed to his daughter.

But he didn't just go to opening night. He and Patience went to every performance. There, in seat G7, the man with the leathery neck and the sunburnt face watched, his eyes glowing not at the drama before him, but at the wonder and magic of letting a thing go and discovering a person gained.

Cage-free

is a mindset

not a method.

21

A Sigh in the Henhouse

The chickens certainly got wind of this play business. Why was the farmer, who normally never ventured out on an evening, suddenly gone night after night?

Juanita clucked, "Bad enough we have to be caged up and restricted. Now he's left us. He doesn't care about us at all."

Why was she complaining that a man she didn't care for didn't care? Strange was this twisted chicken logic. "It all just smells a little foul to me," she clucked.

Boy did that last comment bring a cackle down the line. Oaths and reprimands doodled forth. For—confound it!—there isn't a chicken around who refers to anything as "foul." In the book of chicken protocol, that is #8 in the top 10 things you just never say.

"For pullet sakes!" Peggy cackled. "Have some respect for the species."

Juanita shuddered, losing more than a few feathers down to the quill. What was she thinking? She knew better than to utter that word. *What a birdbrain,* she muttered to herself, pecking her little head convulsively against the wooden bars of her cage.

Not only had Juanita cadoodled herself into a veritable egg constipation, she had lost more than a few feathers since Farmer

Able had cooped up her and the other hens in their tiny workspace prisons.

After yet another worrisome night, she squawked the next morning, "I'm sure I'm just a molted mess. I just know it." Of course, there was no pond or even puddle to provide a mirrored reflection. But any hen certainly knows when her feathers are ruffled.

The other hens were naturally in agreement. Their plumage, though that of simple yardbirds, was a point of pride (certainly not like their relatives the proud peacocks, but in a more humble chickenly fashion). Even as she watched yet another feather come untethered, Juanita squawked, "Heaven help me! I might as well be scalded and plucked!"

It was about that time when the henhouse door opened. The chickens instinctively retreated to the very back of their cages, fearing Foreman Ryder had come. But it was Farmer Able who stood at the doorway. The momentary relief they felt was quickly overridden by yet another panic. *Uh oh. What lame-brained idea does Mr. Advanced Farmer have this time?*

Their fears weren't abated when the farmer strode up and down the coop counting as he went.

Finally Juanita couldn't stand the suspense any further and let out an unchecked stream of squawking. "I'll lay more eggs. I'll push harder. The Egyptians called us 'the bird that gives birth every day'. I promise I'll do that! Cluckadoodle, I will."

A chorus of reprimands from the other hens immediately followed that outburst. "Pipe down you big chicken liver," Peggy clucked. (She hadn't understood the Egyptian reference, summing it up as just another zany idea Juanita liked to steep herself in.)

Peggy continued to try and get Juanita to shut her beak. "You want him to clip our wings even more? Smaller cages? A darker henhouse? Might as well just have him dredge us in flour and throw us in the fryer."

Boy, did that last comment create a stir. Forget the book of chicken protocol; every chicken knows that's a "don't-even-go-there" proposition.

Yet when the farmer had finished his counting, he offered something the chickens hadn't ever heard: a sigh. His compulsive number crunching had finally done some good. No, he wasn't tallying egg production. He was counting his flock. He said out loud, "Whew! Good thing those coyotes didn't carry any of you off."

The farmer had heard some coyotes off in the distance the night before. He wondered if they had come closer and gotten in through a side door that someone had mistakenly left open.

This concern was so unexpected that some thought the farmer's wits had flown the coop. "What did he say? What? What?" Juanita nervously cackled.

Her little cheep actually caught Farmer Able's attention. He moved toward her cage.

"There you've done it, you flufflehead," Peggy scolded.

"Absolutely!" another hen named Madge concurred. "A good chicken never draws the attention of the boss. Just keep your clucker to yourself and do your job."

Farmer Able unhooked and opened Juanita's cage. "Bwackity . . . bwack . . . bwack!!" Juanita said, pushing up against the back of her cage as hard as she could. She hid her head in the corner thinking if she couldn't see him, he couldn't see her. The farmer reached in and grabbed her anyway. She trembled badly. "My only solace is that I might be roasted and not turned into a fricassee," she clucked, sure that this was the end.

But Farmer Able didn't carry her off. No, he actually stroked her a few times, pausing to note, "What's making you lose your feathers, old girl." Juanita didn't like the "old girl" comment, but given the general intent she could abide it.

The farmer paused from his petting and scratched his own head. He looked around at the other chickens, who had all pressed forward in their cages and were looking at him with wide eyes and tipped heads.

"I reckon …" the farmer said out loud, but then paused to cogitate a bit more. Then he strode to the henhouse door.

"That's it. She's soup now!" Peggy couldn't help but exclaim. The other chickens bwacked for Peggy to be still, for Farmer Able stopped just outside the henhouse door.

"I reckon …" he finally finished his thought, "I've been the fool here." And with that he gently let Juanita down on the barnyard ground. She was so stunned—and frankly didn't have her lot legs—that for a moment she just stood there.

"Go on," Farmer Able intoned. "You don't need to be in that cage any more. Heck, I'd lose my feathers, too, if someone confined me like that."

Juanita stared back at him, not understanding that last comment given the featherless— and frankly quite ugly—nature of his skin.

"Go on," he said yet again. "That *Advanced Farmer* magazine be darned! And Willis Achbaucher be danged! And my standing with all those clodhoppers down at the grain elevator be doggoned! Go on, my feathered friend. Be free!"

"Yes, git!" Peggy and the others clucked, straining to see out the door. "Git while the gittin's good."

Juanita finally stopped being paralyzed and stepped her jaunty way further out into the barnyard. Of course, she couldn't help herself. She hadn't gone but a few strides when she saw a fat, little worm sunning himself. "Bless you," Juanita clucked right before she took a gobble. Juanita always remembered to say bless you to the worms for providing themselves so graciously.

Farmer Able's henhouse-cleaning wasn't finished. No, he spent the good part of the morning, flinging open cages and freeing every one of those birds. It certainly did his heart good. But for the chickens . . . well the uncoopiness was so expansive that wouldn't you know, there were enough eggs dropped that day to put a custard factory in a frenzy.

A liberated chicken

makes more eggs.

22

I Am Chicken

Later that afternoon, when Foreman Ryder came up from the fields he was met by all manner of barnyard flutter. Talk about chickens ruling the roost! His first reaction was to ball-out Ernie for leaving the henhouse door open. Ryder raged at him to round up all the renegade chickens.

Ernie had a hen under each arm, and was chasing others, when Farmer Able emerged from the barn. "No, let 'em run," he said. "A bird needs to stretch its wings." Farmer Able went on to explain his new emancipation plan to Ryder and Ernie. "A liberated chicken will feel free to make more eggs."

Ryder was none too happy about it. The foreman had scoffed when the farmer initially told him about his strategy to coop up the chickens, thinking that approach was stupid. But now he rebuffed the farmer exactly because he was undoing that very strategy.

Clarice, who was watching their exchange from the back barn lot, said, "Only content to be a malcontent. Such is Ryder's nature." For if anyone knew about being disgruntled, it was Clarice. Velma and the other cows mooed agreement. They all hated Ryder, but hadn't even realized that in many ways they had become like the man they despised. Velma even added what she thought was an edifying bit of enlightenment, "Yep, sour can be sweet."

"No, sour is power," Louis the cat chimed in from just outside the fence.

"I'm in no mood to hear the musings of a smart aleck cat," Velma snorted.

"I'm just sayin'. You cows just love pooh-mooing everything. Makes you feel important. You'd think you'd know bull dung when you see it."

Bob the bull heard this comment and saw red. He was of a mind to ram the fence and get at that cat, as was the whole herd. But Louis just sauntered off. He paused a few yards away, sat down and licked his paw casually.

"That cat just loves to spite us," Velma moaned.

But Louis' little barb, as prickly as it was, had a certain effect on Clarice. Was she in fact simply a pooh-mooer? Was being sour some kind of sweet thing—some way of getting back at the farmer and the foreman who ruled over them? She wished right then a big four-stomacher would rumble up, because boy did all of these thoughts make her feel gassy. But unfortunately, the fume of all this remained down inside. *I'm a ruminant and I can't even puzzle it out,* she thought. But chew or no chew, Clarice was thinking Louis was on to something. Perhaps she had misjudged things.

Foreman Ryder remained on the warpath. He wasn't pondering nothin'. No, he was downright despising. It irked him that those flappy chickens flitting all over the barn lot reflected a system out of control.

Juanita and the others sure sensed this. They by no means flaunted it. But there was a flap and a flutter to get out of the way when they saw Ryder coming. And now, cageless, they could elude him, which irked him even more.

Farmer Able certainly picked up on Ryder's fuming. He tried to reason with his foreman. "Look Ryder, egg production is down. The cages aren't working. And the pen didn't work before that. Let's give this approach a chance. After all, for centuries chickens were free to wander around and things were just fine. What do you say?"

As he offered this, Farmer Able could feel that gentle wind blowing. Could the buckram foreman sense it?

No. All Ryder thought was *the old man's gone as soft as cottage cheese.* Ryder was determined to harden things back up. "What about the coyotes every night?" Ryder countered. "Those chickens will be easy pickings."

"We'll just have Ernie round them up in the evenings and put them back in the henhouse," Farmer Able said. "They'll be safe."

"Well that's just great. More work for us, and we still don't have the planting done."

The chickens were all listening to this exchange with cocked heads. The word "coyote" certainly quivered their quills. "Ryder's got a point," Peggy quipped. "Those cages, as much as we hate them, are our protection. I'm certainly not going to bwack at Ryder's concern."

There was a lot of anxious cackling from all quarters. The hens started to question the very flapping and fluttering that was so freeing.

Peggy, who had been sunning herself, suddenly thought the light wasn't so enlightening. She rationalized things: "I could keep up my egg production just fine there in the dark. Why was I complaining? I had it so good back in my cage."

Madge could stand it no longer and squawked, "I don't want to be coyote supper!" And she scurried back into the henhouse.

As Peggy continued to pontificate, the whole flock started to falter. They actually thought they saw coyotes behind every shadow. Ryder's fears had become theirs.

However, at that moment a miracle happened. Juanita watched Farmer Able still trying to persuade Ryder. The farmer was standing firm for them!

Seeing this allowed her to see beyond herself and discover her true nature—deep down, just yonder past her gizzard. Yes, Juanita—the one who had allowed her mind to be only as large as her cage, who had found solace in a lowly dirt smudge—remembered those chicken dreams she'd had. Suddenly, she flapped her wings and pushed out her chicken breast.

Normally no chicken ever wants to show a farmer the plumpness of her pectorals, knowing that a human might start imagining certain roasting methods. But chest thumping was exactly what Juanita felt right then.

"Hold your horses, just a cluckity minute," she squawked. (Harry and the other horses were initially more than a bit upset that she was appropriating one of their exclusive phrases, but seeing her courage they allowed it.)

Emboldened, Juanita ran as fast as her chicken legs would allow and placed herself squarely at the henhouse door. "Don't do it!" she exclaimed.

"What's wagging your wattles?" Peggy countered. "You of all hens should know. Those cages are our sanctuary."

Juanita, madder than a wet hen, fluffed her feathers with a certain righteous indignation. "Listen you dumb clucks. Don't you see? The farmer's giving us a chance to spread our wings."

"Maybe if you're a barn swallow, that works," Peggy squawked. "But we're domesticated birds. Flight has never been our forte. And don't you think the coyotes know this. Get away from that doorway and let us get back to what we do best."

"And by that you mean . . ." again Juanita plumped up, ". . . get back to being a bunch of chickens?!"

A gasp went up from the flock. In the book of chicken protocol, this was the #1 "don't go there." Oh, how they were derided by all the other barnyard animals and the humans labeling them as such. They were the laughingstock, the epitome of all things measly and cowardly—but woe to the chicken who ever called herself or her fellow hens this. Yet that is exactly what Juanita did.

Understandably, her admonition was met with silence. For a moment, the hens didn't know what to do. Behind them was the darkened henhouse with its compromised confines. Before them was the wide open but unknown world of the barnyard.

Looking over at Farmer Able still trying to convince Ryder, Juanita added, "Let's trust the man who wants to make things right. He'll put us in at night. He'll keep the coyotes away. He might have made the cages, but now he's willing to see the error of his ways and respect our chicken liberties."

Inspired, Juanita went one step further. Her impassioned clucking rang out like a rallying cry. "Are we barnyard chickens or do we soar like eagles? (She knew this was a stretch but went with the imagery anyway.) As for me, I say, 'I am chicken hear me bwack.'"

Boy, did that stir the hens right in the old gizzard. "Bwww-wackity, bwwack, bwack!" they suddenly cried out in a flurry of fluffed feathers, straining their giblets with glee!

Juanita's clarion call continued to waft out over the hens. It is said that on that day, their quills stopped quivering and their combs got just a little straighter. They turned from the dim doorway of the henhouse and made their way back out into the cage-free sunshine around them.

As Juanita saw the flock unfettered, she calmly exhaled and peeped to herself: *Yep, if you show a little respect and care for others, you might just unlock a boldness as courageous as a chicken.*

Listening
from the heart
unlocks the vast
potential in others.

23

Listening to Be Heard

Ryder left, still in a smolder. Ernie came up to Farmer Able carrying a basketful of eggs. "Isn't it egg-citing?!" he beamed. "I always knew the little cadoodlers had it in 'em."

Farmer Able remembered that Ernie had always been a bit of a chicken whisperer. He conversed in chickenese, claiming to hear all the clucky complaints in the henhouse.

Despite ruffling Ryder's feathers, the good farmer was happy with all these new goin's on. He wanted more. That night when he plopped down in his office chair, the wind was quick to give it. A message came whistling through the knothole: *Trust is a must.*

The farmer jotted this down in his ledger book beneath the other missives. He was starting to have quite a list. The great joy of it was that these blue-sky inspirations were replacing his red-ink computations.

This latest breath of insight, like the others, had to be figured out. One thought immediately came to mind as he focused on the difference between these airy phrases and his hard-pencil numbers: *Trust costs nothing and expands everything.* (Well, he couldn't take full credit for this revelation because the wind continued to blow in a veritable gale of fresh ideas.)

He remembered those emancipated chickens flapping around the barnyard. For certain, it hadn't cost him anything to liberate the hens to be themselves . . . to be free to produce.

He had no sooner cogitated on this than he saw the ants in front of him.

Again as they passed each other, each ant paused to touch feelers. Farmer Able could only imagine what they were saying: *Beware of that big dip just over the desk edge. Queen says, "Sweet! Keep up the good work." Loved playing king of the hill last night! Go 1,546 steps right and 694 steps left then eureka: the sugar! Manufacturing claims they're low on raw materials. How are Uncle Lyle and Baby Anita? Here, can I help you with that load?* Or maybe simply . . . *What a beautiful day!* with a *hi-ya* tacked on for good measure.

Was there a better way to make "trust a must"?

Imagine if I did that with every single soul I came in contact with? the farmer thought.

He had another breezy notion blow through: *All this talk of ants leads to better action. But more importantly, their listening is the best way to be heard.* Astounded by the sheer marvel of it, Farmer Able said out loud, "Is it any wonder that these miniscule mighties build kingdoms that rival the empires of the world?!"

Farmer Able awoke the next day with a new charter. "Good morning, Clarice," he said as he approached her with the milker. "How udderly creamy you're looking today." What inspired him to say this particular line, he didn't know. But something told him that to tell a heifer she had a buttery complexion is in fact the greatest compliment.

Then the farmer did the strangest thing that the whole herd would chew on for the better part of the afternoon. Sitting on the milk stool, he leaned over and placed his ear on Clarice's side.

Clarice was immediately nervous. "He's listening for gastronomic gurgles," she mooed. "If I have another four-stomacher right now, it's off to the meat market I'm sure. The days of cream and sunshine will be over!"

"How you feeling today Clarice?" the farmer asked. Taking a cue from Ernie, Farmer Able was trying to "listen."

"Well if that doesn't butter my toast," Velma said. "What's gotten into the man?"

Clarice was still jumpy.

"Don't have a cow, Clarice," a voice came from just beyond the stanchions. It was Louis. "Darn you, cat! Hush!" Velma mooed. "There wouldn't be a drop of milk for you if it weren't for us."

"And there wouldn't be a lick of sense, if it weren't for me," Louis countered. "C'mon Clarice. Don't you see green clover when it's under hoof?"

Clarice did pause to let all this resonate. Clover had given her indigestion of late. But now she could sense a sudden hankering for it. She let this sink in, right down through all four stomachs. With the farmer's ear still resting on her furry side, the dreaded four-stomacher never came.

What was happening? First her compulsive chewless chewing had abated. And now all that gassy glugging was gone. (Later that night, Clarice would have the most stupendous dream, thinking her cream had won first place in the county butter competition. It was a sweet dream that caused her to lick her lips and smile even as she dozed.)

Farmer Able continued listening, even with his eyes. When he cinched up Harry's harness, he could see the horse telling him something wasn't right. The farmer gave him a gentle pat. "Too snug? Wouldn't want a leather sore." He took the girth strap back a notch. "How's that, boy?"

This crumb of caring actually put Harry in a bit of a bind. He cynically nickered, "I reckon whip-cracking has been replaced by sweet-talking."

"And what's wrong with that?" Jay countered.

"Ahh horse feathers," was all Harry said, yet he had enough horse sense to know a new spirit was in the air.

"Hello chickens," Farmer Able said as he let them out of the henhouse. "Top of the morning to you."

Ricardo the rooster got his hackles up over this, because the farmer was stealing his line. But the hens felt just the opposite. Madge spoke for them all when she clucked, "That old rooster can just crow 'til he's hoarse. If a farmer wants to give us a sunrise greeting, then so be it."

(Ricardo was quite the showman. He wanted everyone to hear his morning wake-up calls and they were delivered with an air of self-importance. He would often keep crowing for a good 30 minutes, even after everyone was awake. Such is the ego of a rooster. When someone thinks they have something to crow about, they often have taken themselves a bit too seriously.)

Conversely, Farmer Able's salutation was genuinely bona fide, especially since it was backed up by his new open door policy. Yes, the chickens were starting to trust him again.

The barn doors of trust were starting to open all around the farm. Jay suggested that the horses could let down their guard as Farmer Able was behind their team.

Harry was all snorty about that idea, not wanting to believe the farmer had their best interests at heart. "A horse pulls," Harry said with disdain. "A farmer doesn't pull. He might lift, and he might heave, but he doesn't pull."

Yet, wouldn't you know it, later that week the horses came into the barn lot and there was Farmer Able "pulling" a cart full of sawdust, and that sawdust was a fresh replenishment for their very stalls.

"Look who's pulling now," Jay couldn't help but nicker. And when a team of horses sees the boss pulling, it gives them a yearning to hit the traces even harder.

Jay even came up with a little horseplay that would make the days go easier and smoother. Which of them could pull the best? It was a veritable muscle-fest as the giant Belgians attempted to out heave-ho the other.

"You game, Harry?" Jay challenged. Harry was about to do his normal *harrumph*, but then he figured something. "That whip might never come back out if I pull hard ..."

"Excuse me, if WE pull harder," Jay interrupted.

And off they went pulling together like never before.

Farmer Able was quick to encourage this effort. Seeing that the fields were getting plowed a little faster, a sweet idea flashed: *I reckon those horses could stand a little molasses on their oats.* So when Harry and the others returned to their stalls that night, what should greet them but the pungent delight of blackstrap-kissed grain. Boy, did they chomp this down.

Ryder remained sour to all this mutual give-and-give. He grew even more agitated. His *do-what-I-say* hounding was being replaced by what he saw as *let-me-do-for-you* hogwash—and heavens, did that chafe his chaps.

He always ballyhooed about production being down and the fields not getting planted. Yet when things started to turn around, he still bellowed. Oddly, the more this whorl of shared respect swirled upward, the more Ryder spiraled downward. He just didn't get it. Losing his grip on those under him was causing him to lose his grip on himself.

Farmer Able kept trying to win him over, but the foreman couldn't abide it.

One day when Ryder brought Harry and the team up from the field, Farmer Able noticed their jaunty step that had started to emerge had been replaced by their old push-pull plodding. They came into the barn lot all lathered up and heads hanging.

Farmer Able immediately knew that something was off. The combination of cleaned-out stalls, molasses-coated oats, and an un-cinched harness had created a bit of horse heaven. It had been working, but now the work was out of the horse.

Ryder complained that they'd only plowed half an acre that day. He was quick to point at what he saw was the blame: "You spoil a horse and it takes the giddy-up out of their go."

Farmer Able knew the unspoken intent of Ryder's griping. "The whip's not coming back out," the farmer said.

"Hey, do you see me carrying a whip?" Ryder said with an air of insult.

As Farmer Able unbuckled their harness, he paused. His anger swelled. "The trouble with you, Ryder, is you think there's a lot of clod in this hopper." And with that, Farmer Able yanked back the harness, revealing fresh whip marks.

Ryder had lied to him.

The foreman lashed out at the farmer. "Those aren't kid's ponies or fancy buggy horses," he said. "They're work horses. And work they'll do as long as I'm running things."

"Well that's just the problem," Farmer Able replied. "You can't run things when you run over them. And I reckon it's time you move along. Don't let the barn door hit you on the way out."

Ryder turned on his heel and left, never to return.

Harry and the other horses stood whinnyless. Was this really happening? Finally, Harry simply nickered as he watched Ryder drive away: "You can lead some humans to water, but you can't make them think."

About that time Ernie came up from the field. He had the whip. Ryder had ditched it in a fencerow just before coming into the barn lot.

Farmer Able took the whip and locked it in a large tack trunk. He pulled out some salve from the same trunk. As he rubbed salve on the horses, he said, "Some people might try to hide a whip, but they can't hide the effect of it."

Ernie, who was helping administer the balm, said, "Been better if Ryder would have whipped his outlook into shape."

How you grow

the harvest

is more important

than the

harvest itself.

24

A Most Earnest
Proposal

That evening, as Farmer Able walked back toward the house, the gentle wind kicked up again. He sensed a bouquet in the air as the wind swirled through the blossoming orchard and then encircled him. He had never noticed that sweet smell before. He had operated like old man Guthrie often quipped, "If you put your head down, get your back under it and keep your nose to the grindstone, that's a pretty uncomfortable and unproductive way to work." Now with his newfound freedom, those trees brought a fragrant new promise.

Things were not just looking up on the farm. No, they were growing broader, wider and deeper. Farmer Able wasn't tallying life simply by pound, bushel and acre. The wind offered a new yard-stick to measure things: *The way to grow the harvest was more important than the harvest itself.*

There it was, plain and simple. Every drop of milk produced, every field plowed, every egg laid—even every kernel of wheat or corn grown—meant nothing, if the way it was achieved was wrong. The greatest yield came from the nobility inspired in every hoof, horn, hand and feather.

As these thoughts whirled around him, brought on by the wind and the perfume of apple blossoms, the farmer smiled a knowing smile.

He heard another breathy utterance: *Ours is yours.* This he did not have to think about. Farmer Able knew immediately what it meant.

The next day he went straightaway to Ernie. "I was mistaken about the chickens," he said.

"Ohhh-kaaaay," Ernie said, knowing this was true but not feeling it was his right to fully endorse the point.

"And I had the wrong idea about how to get the horses stepping out as a team."

"Well ..."

"Go on. You can agree I had blinders on. But hopefully I'm seeing things more clearly now."

"You do see a lightning bug best in the dark," Ernie said.

Farmer Able had to smile at Ernie's insight. "You were illuminated in a lot of this before I was. Now I need to fan that flame."

"Ohh-keedoke," Ernie said, not sure where the farmer was going.

"What I'm saying Ernie is this: I want to put you in charge."

"In charge? Of what?"

"Of making things . . . the way things oughta be. Bringing out their best."

Ernie was a bit intimidated by the idea of taking the lead.

"You certainly know your stuff," the farmer urged. "And you also have heart."

Ernie perked up. "Actually, I've always just followed my nose. That's what a horse does. And a cow for that matter."

Clarice and Harry, who were listening to this exchange, glanced over at each other. They'd never really agreed on anything.

But when you have two eyes staring out over schnozzles as big and commanding as theirs, what Ernie said made perfect sense.

"I want to incentivize you, too."

"I like that word," Ernie said.

"You keep that egg output rollin' in, I'll give you a share. You figure the best way and make the changes necessary to get those fields planted and growing, and I'll share some of the harvest."

"I appreciate the generosity, but that's sure going to cost you."

"Not really. The way my new pencil figures it, I'm giving you part of an increase that wouldn't be there if you hadn't increased it. Do you understand?"

"Yes, sir. It's like what grandma Flora Belle always told her pickers when she paid them based on output. She'd rather have 90% of somethin' than 100% of nothin'."

"Yep, but I don't want to stop there. Let's open up this cistern to the wider world."

When this phrase "the wider world" came out of Farmer Able's mouth, this Old Dirt shook. It wasn't an earthquake. It was just rumbling applause. The cows, horses and chickens felt it, too. But it didn't stop there. Farmer Able wanted it to ripple far and wide . . . out from his acreage . . . to the county . . . from farm to shining farm. Because when a human agrees with the larger workings of the universe, it just can't help but resound with hearty agreement.

At that moment, Farmer Able was surely no longer fixed on that navel he had been so intently gazing at. Now, he was listening to the beat of his heart—a heart expanding at such a rapid rate it had burst beyond the barnyard. His 150 acres couldn't even begin to hold it.

Ernie sparked immediately. "Are we talking about offering a helping hand to others?"

"To be sure. And I want you to have a sayso in that, too."

So from that day forth, as things continued to grow, Farmer Able put a percentage of the harvest in a special goodwill granary. He told Ernie, Patience and Sunny and heck, he even whispered it to the horses, cows and chickens—that they could give the proceeds of the goodwill granary to family and friends in need.

"Heavens to Betsy," Clarice mooed upon hearing this news.

Velma and all the rest of the herd knew what Clarice was referring to once she said Betsy. For that old cow—God rest her soul—always had a bountiful benevolence for the hurting in the herd.

Velma remained dubious. "Farmer Able can talk until the cows come home about Betsy benevolence," she grumbled. "I'll believe it when these brown eyes see it."

Ernie took the first step to take up what the farmer had put down. Always having his lobe bent toward the livestock, he knew there was one thing that was a cow's greatest concern: their calves.

As with all milking operations, the little mooers were held apart from their mommas and kept in their own pen. It's for their own good. Because a Jersey cranks out the creamiest milk, suckling calves will drink and drink until . . . well . . . they have more than a perpetual tummyache.

However, Ernie knew the separation of momma and baby was particularly painful. "It's perfectly preposterous that little Oliver and baby Genevieve are penned up in that pen," he often heard Clarice moan.

"If that doesn't curdle my milk," Velma added, and all the cows certainly agreed.

"I hear ya," Ernie said.

Ernie went to Farmer Able. He not only told the farmer they needed to bring momma and baby together for a time each day, but the calf pens were quite restrictive. "You reckon that goodwill granary fund could be used to rectify this?"

Farmer Able smiled.

So that's how it was, that on a summer day, Ernie came home from the lumber yard and built out not only an expanded pen, but a whole fenced-in pasture for the young-uns. He took it upon himself to bring momma and calf together each day for a little Jersey cream and a lot of momma love.

Even Velma's "why-I-never" turned into wide-eyed delight.

It's no mystery that the share of the harvest that went into the goodwill granary that fall and for years to come just kept getting bigger and bigger. There was so much that Farmer Able and Ernie had to keep expanding the granary just to hold it all. Of course, it never stayed long, because there was always a hurting neighbor near or far who needed help.

Goodness
always seeds
more goodness.

25

The Commitment
of Pigs

The farm became one big circle of life. In a sense, it followed the rhythm of the ants: going out to retrieve and coming back to enrich, which of course led to more going out.

Farmer Able bought a new dog. The cows were initially more than a little concerned, but this time the farmer made sure he had the right dog. He visited several farms. He would test out the dog, observing to make sure it didn't come with any baggage. Yup, this new dog had kindness as part of his pedigree. Farmer Able even named him Easy, because the dog lay back when he brought in the herds. The cows and horses actually came to look forward to seeing Easy, because he made coming up from the field fun. Clarice even said, "Isn't this a dog's life?" Of course, Velma responded, "I wouldn't go that far."

Patience continued to plant her seeds of kindness, only now they took root within her husband. Over time she saw him continue to transform as the hard ground in his life became rich and fertile. The man she had always appreciated reemerged with a gentle strength that continued to delight her. And those dishes never were cleaner.

Sunny matured like a summer garden, generous and bountiful. The generosity of spirit returned between father and daughter. Overall, the sunshiny outlook in her life grew even brighter. She had always been sensitive to the chickens, but now as she hunted for eggs, she became a bit of a chicken whisperer herself, thanks to Ernie's example. Gosh darn if Juanita and the others didn't tell her with so many clucks how fortunate they were to be free to range and roam. Boy did it bring an unexpected smile when they intimated how her dad was such an inspiration.

Farmer Able realized a timeless paradox. When you make a second thing first, you not only lose the second thing, you lose the first thing, too. Work is supposed to be the second thing and family first. By switching the order of importance, he nearly lost them both. Now that things were put in proper order—family first and work second—he truly had gained both in all their fullness.

Clarice was certainly happy. Gone for good were the dark days of her cud-chewing disorder. Any four-stomacher she felt presently was a belch of gladness, for as Louis had said, her hoofs were certainly standing in clover. Velma came to realize that the fresh straw that tickled the cows' noses and comforted them during their sleeping was better than that "deep warmth" of the manure pile. Heck, the whole herd became Jersey proud again and started churning out milk in record amounts. Clarice stopped being resentful about the bell around her neck and now wore it with a sense of belonging; its gentle tones rang in a joy that felt good. Yes, these indeed were the days of alfalfa and butter!

Harry stopped his neigh-saying and boy did he and the other steeds pull up a storm. The big Belgians were actually upset when the spring planting was done—accomplished in record time. Yeah, they enjoyed the lazy days of summer, but they couldn't wait until they could help bring in the fall harvest. Harry even nickered, "Work has become horseplay."

Juanita and the chickens were absolutely feather-pated by their new free-range arrangement. She squawked one day, "Better than any chicken dream." And with that she was so excited she popped out yet another egg. Juanita became such a stellar producer that by summer's end she was given the award for "Best Yolk Achievement," voted unanimously by all the hens.

And the pigs . . . well they continued to do what they always did: eat, lay in the shade and grow fat. As the attitudes of all things hoofed and horned, feathered and fleshed brightened, it slowly dawned on each one of them that the pigs were in fact making the greatest contribution. For as they say, when it comes to a ham-and-egg breakfast, a chicken is involved but a pig is committed. Or as Farmer Able said one day as he sat on his porch and surveyed all the bounty before him, "The pigs were never running the farm at all. It was our own hoggish behavior."

Don't you think this Old Dirt didn't notice all this. I even took it upon myself to urge Cedric Raincloud and even Isabelle Sun to work together with me to bring forth an extra bounty of crops. Goodness always seeds more goodness. Of course, that very muck Farmer Able had spread on the fields also worked its magic, proving that awfulness can even be turned into gain. No one needs the wind to tell 'em that.

As for the wind . . . it did what wind always does: continue to blow its many virtues to any of a mind to hear its wisdom, feel its transforming peace and ride it to the stars.

THE END

CPSIA information can be obtained at www.ICGtesting.com
Printed in the USA
BVOW05s0205130215

387566BV00002B/22/P